WRITERS AND TF

ISOBEL ARMST
General Edi

JONATHAN SWIFT

JONATHAN SWIFT

JONATHAN SWIFT

Ian Higgins

NORTHCOTE
BRITISH
COUNCIL

© Copyright 2004 by Ian Higgins

First published in 2004 by Northcote House Publishers Ltd, Horndon, Tavistock, Devon, PL19 9NQ, United Kingdom.
Tel: +44 (01822) 810066. Fax: +44 (01822) 810034.

British Library Cataloguing-in-Publication Data
A catalogue record for this book is available from the British Library

ISBN 0-7463-1105-2 hardcover
ISBN 0-7463-0782-9 paperback

Typeset by TW Typesetting, Plymouth, Devon
Printed and bound in the United Kingdom by
Athenaeum Press Ltd., Gateshead, Tyne & Wear

For Elaine Higgins and for Keswick Higgins,
and in memory of Thelma Pyne.

Contents

Biographical Outline

1667   30 November: Swift born in Dublin to an English father, Jonathan Swift, and a mother of English extraction, Abigail Swift (née Erick).

1673–82   Attends Kilkenny Grammar School.

1682–9   Attends Trinity College, Dublin. BA *speciali gratia* 1686.

1687   James II's Declaration of Indulgence, a prerogative toleration of Protestant Dissenters and Roman Catholic Recusants.

1688   Republication of the Declaration of Indulgence. Anglican opposition to royal policy. Birth of James Francis Edward Stuart, son and heir of James II. William of Orange leads a Dutch invasion of England. James II flees to France.

1688–9   The 'Glorious Revolution'. William and Mary crowned King and Queen by the Convention Parliament. Supporters of the deposed James II and his heirs become known as Jacobites from the Latin *Jacobus*, James. Those who refused the Oath of Allegiance to William and Mary and subsequent post-Revolution monarchs are known as nonjurors. Fighting between Williamite and Jacobite armies in Ireland and Scotland. Swift leaves for England. He joins the household of Sir William Temple, the retired statesman and diplomat at Moor Park in Surrey, becoming his secretary. Swift meets Esther Johnson ('Stella' was then 8 years old). At about this time he experiences the first symptoms of what was to be a lifelong affliction and what later medical authorities have diagnosed as Ménière's syndrome, a disease of the inner ear causing, as in Swift's case, giddiness, nausea, and deafness. The 'Toleration Act' (1689) exempts Protestant Dissenters from penalties for non-attendance at the services of the Established Anglican Church.

1690   Swift returns to Ireland. Battle of the Boyne. Defeat and exile of James II.

1691   Swift publishes first poem, 'Ode. To the King on his Irish Expedition' (Dublin, 1691). Returns to Moor Park. Treaty of Limerick.

1692   Swift receives MA from Hart Hall, Oxford. Publishes 'Ode to the Athenian Society'. Writing an 'Ode to Dr William Sancroft' (begun in 1689).

1693   At Moor Park. Composes an Ode 'To Mr Congreve' intended to be prefixed to Congreve's *The Double Dealer*. Verses by Dryden were prefixed to the published play.

1694   Ordained deacon in the Church of Ireland.

1695–6 Ordained priest (1695). Appointed as prebendary of Kilroot, near Carrickfergus, north of Belfast in County Antrim, an area dominated by Scots Presbyterians. Probably begins work on *A Tale of a Tub* containing a violent satire on fundamentalist Dissent. Friendship with Jane Waring ('Varina') and proposes marriage. Abandons Kilroot in 1696, returns to Moor Park. Jacobite Assassination Plot against William III (1696).

1696–9 At work on the *Tale* while editing Temple's correspondence and memoirs for publication.

1699   Temple dies. Appointed chaplain to Earl of Berkeley, Lord Justice of Ireland. Returns to Dublin.

1700   Swift becomes Vicar of Laracor, County Meath, with a prebend in St Patrick's Cathedral in Dublin.

1701   Returns to England with Berkeley. Publishes *Contests and Dissensions in Athens and Rome* on the side of Berkeley's political party, the Whigs. Esther Johnson and her companion Rebecca Dingley move to Dublin. Swift returns to Dublin. Act of Settlement. James II dies in exile in France. His son, James Francis Edward, the 'Pretender' to the British throne.

1702	Swift becomes Doctor of Divinity, Trinity College, Dublin. Death of William III. Accession of Queen Anne (the last reigning Stuart monarch).
1703	November: leaves Dublin for England, probably with the manuscript of *A Tale of a Tub*.
1704	Publishes *A Tale of a Tub*, *The Battle of the Books*, and *A Discourse concerning the Mechanical Operation of the Spirit*.
1704–7	Swift in Ireland.
1707	Union of England and Scotland. Writes first pamphlet on Ireland, 'The Story of the Injured Lady'.
1707–9	Swift in London as delegate of the Church of Ireland soliciting for the remission of the 'first fruits', a tax on the clergy. Friendship with Addison, Steele, and other writers, and with Esther Vanhomrigh ('Vanessa'). 'The Bickerstaff Papers' (1708–9). Composing pamphlets attacking Whig religious policy. *A Letter . . . concerning the Sacramental Test* (1708), *A Project for the Advancement of Religion* (1709). Returns to Ireland.
1710	September: Swift back in London. Begins *Journal to Stella*. October: the Tories win the general election. Swift agrees to write for Robert Harley and the new Tory government, producing poems and pamphlets excoriating Whig persons, principles, and proceedings. Appointed editor of the ministerial paper the *Examiner* and writes a series of thirty-three weekly essays. Fifth edition of *A Tale of a Tub* with additions and changes.
1711	*Miscellanies in Prose and Verse* (includes *An Argument against Abolishing Christianity*); *The Conduct of the Allies*.
1712	*A Proposal for Correcting the English Tongue*.
1713	Swift made Dean of St Patrick's Cathedral, Dublin (in the gift of the Second Duke of Ormonde not the Queen) and is installed in Dublin. Returns to London and the propaganda war against the Whigs. Scriblerus Club (Swift, Alexander Pope, John Arbuthnot, John Gay, Thomas Parnell, and Robert Harley now Earl of Oxford). Treaty of Utrecht ends war with France.

1714   Death of Queen Anne and collapse of the Tory government. Accession of George I and the House of Hanover. Swift returns to his deanery in Dublin and what he regards as 'exile' in Ireland. Esther Vanhomrigh ('Vanessa') follows him to Ireland, residing at Celbridge near Dublin. After the Hanoverian succession the Tory Party is effectively proscribed from power. Swift is suspected of Jacobitism and his correspondence is opened by postal officers.

1715   Impeachment of Tory leaders Bolingbroke, Ormonde, and Oxford on charges of Jacobite conspiracy. Jacobite rebellion in Scotland.

1715–20 Swift in 'retirement' in Ireland during what was, for Swift, a Hanoverian Whig reign of terror: 'for many years he was worried by the new people in power, and had hundreds of libels writ against him in England' (note in Faulkner edition of *Verses on the Death of Dr Swift*).

1720   South Sea Bubble. Declaratory Act asserts British Parliament's right to legislate for Ireland. Swift, *A Proposal for the Universal Use of Irish Manufacture*. Jacobite conspiracy 1720–3 ('the Atterbury Plot').

1721–42 Robert Walpole Prime Minister.

1721–5 Swift at work on *Gulliver's Travels*.

1723   Death of Vanessa.

1724   *The Drapier's Letters*, opposing a patent granted by the Crown to William Wood to manufacture copper coinage for Ireland. Swift achieves a popular reputation as an Irish patriot.

1726   Swift travels to London with the manuscript of *Gulliver's Travels*. Unproductive meeting with Walpole on the subject of Ireland. *Cadenus and Vanessa*, Swift's longest poem, published. *Gulliver's Travels* published after Swift leaves for Dublin.

1727   Swift's final visit to London. The first of the Swift–Pope *Miscellanies* is published. Death of George I, accession of George II.

1728   Death of Stella. *A Short View of the State of Ireland*. Swift and Thomas Sheridan collaborate on the periodical the *Intelligencer*.

1729	*A Modest Proposal.*
1731	Composes *Verses on the Death of Dr Swift.*
1733	Swift, 'On Poetry: A Rhapsody'.
1735	George Faulkner's Dublin edition of Swift's *Works* in 4 volumes (volume 3 contains a revised text of *Gulliver's Travels*).
1736	Swift, 'The Legion Club'.
1737	Swift, *A Proposal for Giving Badges to the Beggars.* Swift's last pamphlet on Ireland and, unusually, Swift signed the work.
1738	Swift, *A Complete Collection of Genteel and Ingenious Conversation.*
1739	*Verses on the Death of Dr Swift* published.
1742	Aged 75 Swift is declared 'of unsound mind and memory'.
1744	Death of Alexander Pope.
1745	Death of Swift on 19 October at the Deanery of St Patrick's in Dublin. His Will includes a request to be buried in the Cathedral 'as privately as possible, and at Twelve o'Clock at Night' and a bequest for the foundation of St. Patrick's Hospital for 'as many Idiots and Lunaticks' as can be maintained. *Directions to Servants* published. Death of Walpole. Death of 2nd Duke of Ormonde. Jacobite Rebellion.

Abbreviations and References

Corr.   *The Correspondence of Jonathan Swift*, ed. Harold Williams, 5 vols. (Oxford, 1963–5)

CW   *The Correspondence of Jonathan Swift, D.D.*, ed. David Woolley, 4 vols. (Frankfurt am Main, 1999–)

Poems *Jonathan Swift: The Complete Poems*, ed. Pat Rogers (Harmondsworth, 1983)

PW   *The Prose Writings of Jonathan Swift*, ed. Herbert Davis *et al.*, 16 vols. (Oxford, 1939–74). All quotations from *Gulliver's Travels* are from volume xi of this edition; reference is by part, chapter, and page number (e.g. iv. x. 276)

Swift   Irvin Ehrenpreis, *Swift: The Man, his Works, and the Age*, 3 vols. (London, 1962–83)

Tale   *A Tale of a Tub to which is added The Battle of the Books and the Mechanical Operation of the Spirit*, ed. A. C. Guthkelch and D. Nichol Smith (2nd edn., Oxford, 1958; corrected reprint, 1973)

Biblical references are to the King James Authorized Version.

1

Biography: Priest and Satirist

Jonathan Swift was a priest in the (Anglican) Church of Ireland
and an Irish patriot, a poet, pamphleteer, and the most
powerful prose satirist of his time. Alexander Pope's tribute to
Swift in *The Dunciad* celebrates his fame as priest, patriot, and
satirist, points to his penchant for pseudonymity, and places
him with the greats of European satire:

> O Thou! whatever title please thine ear,
> Dean, Drapier, Bickerstaff, or Gulliver!
> Whether thou chuse Cervantes' serious air,
> Or laugh and shake in Rab'lais' easy chair . . .[1]

Henry Fielding described Swift as a 'Genius who deserves to
be ranked among the first whom the World ever saw. He
possessed the Talents of a Lucian, a Rabelais, and a Cervantes,
and in his Works exceeded them all'.[2] Swift reflected on his
literary achievement and reputation, remarking in a letter of
1732: 'I am conjectured to have generally dealt in Raillery and
Satyr, both in Prose and Verse . . . and charitable People will
suppose I had a Design to laugh the Follies of Mankind out of
Countenance, and as often to lash the Vices out of Practice'
(*Corr.* iv. 53). Swift is the pre-eminent prose satirist in the
English language. He is also a major satiric poet. Swift's
favourite, indeed signature, verse form was the tetrameter
couplet; his satiric verse is characteristically quotidian in its
subject matter, colloquial in diction, and exuberant in its
rhymes. The following chapters in this book focus on the major
satires upon which Swift's literary reputation principally rests:
A Tale of a Tub, *An Argument against Abolishing Christianity*,
Gulliver's Travels, *A Modest Proposal*, and his infamous

'scatological' poems. For many within Swift's first community of readers his provocative polemic and satire implied off-the-page menaces. Swift's satire, for instance, can figuratively kill people, as in the case of John Partridge, victim of a Swiftian satiric assassination in 1708, whose serial murder by premeditated pamphlets is reviewed in this study.

The excoriating power of Swift's writing and the enduring individual and institutional failings that his writing addresses have meant that Swift's satires still speak to modern readers who live in a radically different epoch and who would not share Swift's fundamental assumptions. Swift's most famous work, *Gulliver's Travels*, was a sensational public event on its first publication: 'From the highest to the lowest it is universally read, from the Cabinet-council to the Nursery' (John Gay to Swift, 17 November 1726, *Corr*. iii. 182). It continues to reach vast audiences through print and other media. When Charles Sturridge's television version of *Gulliver's Travels* was originally shown on the NBC television network in the United States on 4 and 5 February 1996, it was said to have had an estimated viewing audience of fifty-six million people. The timeless or universal aspect of Swift's writing can, by definition, be readily understood by readers today. However, Swift's works, even his apparently general satires, have a contextual location and provenance as literary interventions in the paper wars and controversies of his time. The meaning of Swift's works begins to emerge fully only when they are read in relation to the allusive field in which they operate, which includes now-neglected pamphlets and fugitive pieces, as well as the major authors and literary traditions usually adduced in studies of Swift. In this book some prominence is given to perhaps unfamiliar contemporary polemical contexts of Swift's most famous works. Swift's writings have generated a vast corpus of commentary; nevertheless the scholarly recovery of contemporary contexts still affords the prospect of new angles on the interpretation of Swift's major texts. This introductory chapter offers a short account of Swift's life and attempts to identify this priest's signature as satirist and political writer.

Swift was born in Dublin on 30 November 1667. The Swifts were English and Jonathan was the grandson of Thomas Swift, a Royalist Anglican vicar of Goodrich in Herefordshire whose memory Swift venerated and whose militancy in the cause of King Charles I Swift especially celebrated (*PW* v. 188–90, 334). Swift was therefore born into the small Anglo-Irish Anglican establishment in a country with a large Roman Catholic majority and significant Presbyterian minority. Catholic Ireland looked to Rome and the exiled House of Stuart for leadership. Irish Presbyterians looked to Scotland and the Whig Party in England. The Anglican minority tended to reflect the Whig/Tory party-political divisions in England. Whigs perceived Roman Catholicism and Jacobitism as the greatest threat to the Irish establishment. They sought concessions for Protestant Dissenters and Protestant unity in the face of this threat. Tories regarded Protestant Dissenters as the greater menace. Irish High Churchmen, especially during Queen Anne's reign, looked to the Tory or 'Church' Party in London, which seemed to offer the best prospects for the further suppression of Protestant Dissent. In *A Letter from a Member of the House of Commons in Ireland to a Member of the House of Commons in England, concerning the Sacramental Test* (1708) Swift explained that the real threat to Anglican throats came from Protestant Dissenters not from the Catholic Jacobite majority:

> IT is agreed, among Naturalists, that a *Lyon* is a larger, a stronger, and more dangerous Enemy than a *Cat*; yet if a Man were to have his Choice, either a *Lyon* at his Foot, bound fast with three or four Chains, his Teeth drawn out, and his Claws pared to the Quick, or an angry *Cat* in full Liberty at his Throat; he would take no long Time to determine. (*PW* ii. 122)

In the 1720s Swift's pamphleteering against the English government would gain him a deserved reputation as an Irish patriot, but Swift was always something of an isolated figure, both as a patriot and as a member of the Anglo-Irish minority establishment. He was an Irish patriot who nevertheless supported legislation that preserved the hegemony of the Anglican minority by depriving Roman Catholics and Protestant Dissenters from the Established Church of Ireland of full civil rights. For much of his life Swift was disaffected from the small Anglo-Irish establishment to which he belonged by ethnicity and confession, believing that the principles of Whig rule in Ireland 'consisted in nothing else but damning the Church, reviling the Clergy, abetting the Dissenters, and speaking contemptibly of revealed Religion'. The 'whiggish or fanatical Genius so prevalent among the English of this kingdom' was to be accounted for 'by that number of Cromwell's Soldiers, adventurers established here, who were all of the sourest Leven, and the meanest birth, and whose posterity are now in possession of their lands and their principles' (*PW* ix. 30–1). In his most famous satire on Ireland, *A Modest Proposal* (1729), Swift indicts the 'whiggish or fanatical Genius' of the established settler class in the unspeakable 'Modest Proposer' whose barbarism is shared by the native Irish and their English oppressors.

As a high-profile propagandist and apologist for Queen Anne's Tory government of 1710–14 (the leaders of which, Robert Harley, Earl of Oxford, Henry St John, Viscount Bolingbroke, and James Butler, Second Duke of Ormonde, had entered into the service of the Pretender after the Hanoverian accession), Swift was politically isolated in an Ireland under Whig rule after 1714. He was a proscribed man suspected of Jacobitism by the government. Swift's writings on Ireland typically and explosively combine the perspectives of priest, patriot, and Tory polemicist. The priest locates the cause of Ireland's wretched condition in the vices of the Irish themselves. The patriot blames oppressive English policies for Irish poverty. The disaffected Tory identifies the English Whig government and its Irish Whig clients as authors of Ireland's ruin.

Swift's putative father died before he was born and through the generosity of his uncles he was given the best possible education at Kilkenny Grammar School and Trinity College Dublin, both under the strong High Church Tory influence of the Ormonde family. He attended Trinity College until the outbreak of war between Jacobite and Williamite armies in Ireland at the Revolution. Swift left for England, where with his mother's encouragement he entered the household of Sir William Temple at Moor Park in Surrey. Temple was a retired statesman, author, and a friend and adviser of William III. He became Swift's first patron. There has been speculation, however, that Swift was really the natural son of John Temple,

William Temple's father, and that his prestigious education and patronage in Sir William Temple's household and other curious features of his biography might be explained by Temple consanguinity.[3] Alternatively, Swift's first biographer, John Boyle, Fifth Earl of Cork and Orrery, says that 'the general voice of fame' had it that Swift and Esther Johnson were 'the natural children of SIR WILLIAM TEMPLE'.[4] Whatever the truth, Swift worked for Temple as a secretary during the decade 1689–99 (though he returned to Ireland in 1690 and again in 1694–6), editing Temple's memoirs and letters for publication. Swift expected great things from Temple's patronage and connections, but they failed to materialize. At the beginning of his time at Moor Park he experienced the symptoms of Ménière's syndrome, a disease of the inner ear, which was not then understood and which afflicted and distressed him throughout his life. At Moor Park he also met Esther Johnson, then a young girl, who would become a lifelong intimate friend. Some believe they were secretly married. Swift took some part in her education. The playful and historically important correspondence addressed to Esther Johnson (and to her older companion Rebecca Dingley) when he was in London between 1710 and 1713 is known as the *Journal to Stella*. The sequence of birthday poems he addressed to her as 'Stella' (the name was presumably taken from Sir Philip Sidney's famous sonnet sequence *Astrophel and Stella*) are a brilliant testimony to this friendship. Swift, of course, did not write love poems; what others might understand as love, Swift dismissed as 'that ridiculous passion which hath no Being, but in Play-Books and Romances' (*PW* ix. 89). But these bantering and didactic birthday poems, which mock the conventions of love poetry, can be regarded as Swiftian versions of the love lyric. Swift's 'Prayers for Stella' (*PW* ix. 253–7) are a further testament of his friendship. Swift's grief at her death is palpable in his emotionally powerful, heart-broken account 'of the truest, most virtuous, and valuable friend, that I, or perhaps any other person ever was blessed with', which he began writing on the night of her death, 28 January 1728. Swift's account of Stella is all the more moving as he attempts to achieve emotional detachment ('On the Death of Mrs. Johnson', *PW* v. 227–36).

Swift's first writings belong to the early 1690s. He began his literary career as a poet, writing pindaric odes in the manner of Abraham Cowley on affairs of Church and State and on literature. The enigmatic ambiguity of Swift's political stance towards William III in these early writings invites analogy with Cowley's attitude to Cromwell. Cowley's notorious ode 'To Brutus' (1656) can be construed as both Royalist and Republican, as both pro- and anti-Cromwell. Swift's early works apparently display starkly contradictory views of the ruler who had displaced the Stuart king. In 1691 he published an Ode to William III representing the new king as a conqueror and looking to him to crush the enemies of Anglican hegemony ('Ode. To the King on His Irish Expedition, and the Success of His Arms in general. Presented to His Majesty upon His departure from Ireland' (Dublin, 1691); *Poems*, 43–6). He was soon disappointed in William III, whom he later blamed (in anonymous or unpublished writings) for the abolition of episcopacy in Scotland, for overseeing the economic ruin of Ireland, for involving England in expensive war abroad, and for continuing James II's toleration of Dissent. Publicly, *in propria persona*, Swift loyally dedicated Sir William Temple's *Letters* (1700) 'To His Most Sacred Majesty William III' (*PW* i. 256), but anonymously in the 1690s Swift treats the King with sneering scatological derision. In the venomous prose and poetry on affairs of state in the 1690s, Jacobite writers jeered that William had defecated at his coronation.[5] In an early poem entitled 'The Problem' (1699) Swift joined in the anti-Williamite derision: 'We read of kings, who in a fright, | Though on a throne, would fall to shite' (ll.19–20, in *Poems*, 82). There is obscure and unspeakable menace of the militaristic William III in the satiric treatment of King Henri IV of France in the 'Digression on Madness' in *A Tale of a Tub* (written *c*. 1696–7). In the 'Digression on Madness' military conquest is clinically explained as a madness that occurs when the brain is overturned by a vapour. There is a reference to defecation and perhaps an obscure allusion to William III's coronation accident: 'Fumes issuing from a Jakes, will furnish as comely and useful a Vapor, as Incense from an Altar' (*PW* i. 102). The 'Digression on Madness' instances Henri IV as a mad militaristic monarch, but it is William III who seems also to be in the

satirist's sights. The satire apparently approves of the assassination of the militaristic (and tolerationist) monarch 'Harry *the
Great of* France' by 'Ravillac, *who stabb'd* Henry *the Great in his
Coach'*. The effect of the satire is that the disease in the body
politic embodied by 'Henri IV' deserved the cure:

> A certain Great Prince raised a mighty Army, filled his Coffers
> with infinite Treasures, provided an invincible Fleet, and all this,
> without giving the least Part of his Design to his greatest Ministers,
> or his nearest Favourites. Immediately the whole World was
> alarmed . . . In the midst of all these Projects and Preparations; a
> certain *State-Surgeon,* gathering the Nature of the Disease by these
> Symptoms, attempted the Cure, at one Blow performed the
> Operation, broke the Bag, and out flew the *Vapour;* nor did any
> thing want to render it a compleat Remedy, only, that the Prince
> unfortunately happened to Die in the Performance.   (*PW* i. 103)

Swift's satire has a menacing resonance, for, in the contemporary press, the Jacobite Plot of 1696 to kill William III in his
coach was paralleled with the assassination of Henri IV in his
coach by Ravaillac in 1610.[6] That Swift also meant William III
when he wrote about Henri IV might also be revealed by a
verbal echo of the *Tale*'s insouciant passage about 'Henri IV'
('the Prince unfortunately happened to Die') in a passage about
predictions of Jacobite plots against the life of William III in the
first of Swift's mock-astrological 'Bickerstaff Papers' in 1708 ('if
the King should happen to have died' (*PW* ii. 143)).

In the early 1690s Swift wrote an 'Ode to Dr William
Sancroft', the deprived Archbishop of Canterbury, a Stuart
loyalist who nevertheless defied James II in defence of the
Church of England but who refused to take the oaths to
William III. Sancroft was the subject of Anglican Jacobite
hagiography.[7] Swift imagines Sancroft in Heaven 'from arch
-prelate here, | Translated to arch-angel there' (ll. 238–9, in
Poems, 67). Swift said in a letter of 1692 that he was even
willing to come out politically with this poem: 'I would send
it to my Bookseller and make him print it with my name and
all, to show my respect and Gratitude to that excellent person,
and to perform half a Promise I made [Francis Turner, Bishop]
of Ely upon it' (*CW* i. 110; in 1692 the nonjuring Bishop was a
Jacobite outlaw). The 'Ode to Dr William Sancroft' is

7

unfinished. Swift would take the oaths to the king in possession ruling with Parliament, but the young High Churchman in the 1690s, with an uncertain settlement in life, sometimes writes in the language of Jacobite disaffection, the language of the party of dispossessed but respected nonjuring Anglicans with whom Swift was acquainted or whom he admired, men such as Francis Turner, Bishop of Ely, Robert Nelson, and Archbishop Sancroft. His early poetry is politically remarkable in what it discloses of his private views at this time. His 'Ode' to his employer Sir William Temple denounces palaces and courts. An 'Ode to the Athenian Society' and an Ode 'To Mr Congreve' disclose conservative, anti-modern cultural affiliations.

Swift took his MA from Hart Hall at Oxford University in 1692. He returned to Ireland from Moor Park in 1694 and entered the Church of Ireland and was ordained priest in 1695. He was appointed to Kilroot, near Belfast, a Presbyterian heartland. In 1696 he proposed marriage to a Belfast woman, Jane Waring ('Varina'), who initially hesitated. Swift clearly felt rejected and later, in effect, refused to marry her when she was prepared to accept him. This seems to have been a deeply unhappy period of his life. But it was probably at his Anglican outpost surrounded by fundamentalist Dissent that he began *A Tale of a Tub*, the scandalous satire on the Roman Catholic and Dissenting enemies of the Church of England and on the abuses in modern learning. He worked on the *Tale* largely in secret and the work was not published until 1704 and was never publicly acknowledged by Swift. The satire on Roman Catholicism ('popery') earned the work a place in the Vatican's *Index Librorum Prohibitorum*. A principal Whig victim of Swift's satire, William Wotton, in his *Observations upon The Tale of a Tub* in 1705, thought 'the Protestant Dissenters' were 'to outward appearance, the most directly levelled at' (*Tale*, 325) – a view shared by many readers. The sensational work was commonly interpreted as an attack on religion. Swift was to claim in an anonymous 'Apology' affixed to the fifth edition of the book published in 1710 that it attacked abuses in religion. Swift believed that his brilliant early book had prevented his promotion in the Church. Swift's published works during the Moor Park decade and immediately afterwards, such as the

'Ode' to William III, the editing of Temple's writings, and *A Discourse of the Contests and Dissentions between the Nobles and the Commons in Athens and Rome* (1701), a defence of impeached Whig lords, were very different in kind to the *Tale of a Tub* and identified him with the Whigs (the political party regarded as the more sympathetic to Protestant Dissenters) from whom he sought patronage.

After Temple's death in 1699 Swift held appointments in the Church of Ireland. He becomes a Doctor of Divinity at Trinity College, Dublin in 1702. During the years 1699–1710 he was publicly aligned with the Whig Party and his friends included the Whig writers and politicians Joseph Addison and Richard Steele. He contributed to the *Tatler*, publishing there his urban pastoral poems 'A Description of the Morning' (1709) and 'A Description of a City Shower' (1710), and an important essay on the English language (*Tatler*, no. 230, 28 Sept. 1710; *PW* ii. 172–7). He caught the public imagination with his mock-astrological 'Bickerstaff Papers' (1708–9), a brilliantly executed April Fool's Day joke and literary hoax at the expense of the leading London astrologer John Partridge. However, his writings on religion, published and unpublished in this period, reflect his deep disquiet with Whig ecclesiastical policy. His conversion to the Tories (or the 'Church party' as Swift called them), which happened in 1710, reflected his actual ecclesiastical–political allegiance.

Swift's earliest writings on Ireland also belong to the first decade of the eighteenth century. Significantly, the defence of Irish Anglicanism is central to his first pamphlet on Ireland, 'The Story of the Injured Lady. Written by Herself. In a Letter to her Friend, with his Answer' (written in 1707). In this political allegory the injured lady is Ireland, the ungrateful lover is England, and the perfidious rival mistress is Scotland. The pamphlet stridently opposes the proposed Union of England and Scotland (1707) as a betrayal of Ireland, especially of Irish Anglicanism. Not surprisingly, Swift's pamphlet was not published. Swift at this time was still seeking preferment from the English Whigs and the pamphlet's Irish patriotism just happens to coincide with Jacobite and Tory argument. Indeed, hostility to the Union would fuel Jacobitism for the next half century. Swift's allegory complains of England's treatment of Ireland as a colony rather than as an independent kingdom under the same crown, identifying political and economic grievances associated with the Williamite Whig government in Ireland and England. The pamphlet displays Swift's lifelong intense animus against Presbyterian Scotland. 'The Story of the Injured Lady' and 'The Answer to the Injured Lady' are characteristic of Swift's later Irish writings, in that blame is placed on the Irish themselves as well as on their oppressors. The 'Story' focuses on English turpitude and oppression, the 'Answer' concentrates on Irish culpability for the country's plight (PW ix. 1–12).

In 1707 or 1708 Swift met Esther (or Hester) Vanhomrigh. His invented name for her was Vanessa. An intimate friend of Swift's during his years in London, she later followed him to Dublin. Their relationship seems to have been sexual in character (there were certainly declarations of passion on her part) and was conducted like a clandestine adultery with secretive assignations and with the associated silences and lies (or at least suppression of the full truth) about his meetings with Vanessa in his letters to Stella from London. Vanessa died in 1723 apparently estranged from Swift. Swift's version of the happy period of their relationship can be read in his longest poem, Cadenus and Vanessa (written c. 1713), which was not intended for publication. When manuscript copies of the poem began circulating in public, Swift dismissed the poem as 'only a cavalier business' and 'a private humorsome thing' (Corr. iii. 130). It was published in unauthorized editions in 1726. Swift's relationships with Stella and Vanessa have engendered informed speculation and much more myth but no certainty. Swift is not fully revealed in the surviving documentary record.

The period 1710–14 sees Swift writing some of the most powerful poetry and prose ever produced in defence of a government. In 1710 Swift was again in London, commissioned by the Irish bishops to solicit on behalf of the clergy of the Church of Ireland for a remission of financial imposts on the clergy paid to the Crown. This embassy had been thwarted under the Whigs (who wanted concessions made to the Dissenters as the price for this financial relief) but achieved success under Queen Anne's new Tory government led by Robert Harley. Personal dissatisfaction with his treatment by

the Whigs and ecclesiastical–political principle drove Swift
into the arms of the Tories. He began writing for the new Tory
government, producing a series of thirty-three essays for the
Examiner, the ministerial paper. Swift was the government's
brilliant highbrow propagandist, consciously pitching his work
a cut above Grub Street, and appealing to the political nation,
particularly to the government's own constituency, whose
prejudices Swift confirms and inflames for the government's
legislative ends. In prose and poetry Swift arraigned the Duke
of Marlborough, the hero of the pro-War Whig party. He wrote
important pamphlets assassinating the reputation of prominent Whigs such as the Earl of Wharton, Richard Steele, and
Anthony Collins, and powerfully supported the government's
policy of peace with France in *The Conduct of the Allies* (1711).
As government apologist, Swift effectively adopted an Olym-
pian tone in indicting the persons, principles, and proceedings
of the previous Whig government and dictating the new Tory
line. Swift defended the Tory ministry with his person and
penknife as well as his pen. On 4 November 1712 he defused
a letter bomb meant for the Lord Treasurer, Robert Harley, Earl
of Oxford. According to the account of the incident Swift gave
to the government press, he took the suspicious parcel away
from the Tory leader, cut the pack threads with his penknife,
and discovered a gunpowder device of two primed pistols.
This latterday gunpowder plot became known as the Bandbox
Plot. Swift's heroism was duly greeted with derision by Whig
propagandists (*PW* vi. 196–7; *Swift*, ii. 583).

Swift also took part in Tory sociability. He belonged to two
clubs, the Society of Brothers, the High Tory answer to the
Whig elite's Kit-Cat Club, and the Scriblerus Club, a literary
group that included Alexander Pope, John Gay, John Arbuthnot, Thomas Parnell, and Robert Harley, Earl of Oxford. The
great Scriblerian satires of the 1720s – *Gulliver's Travels*, Gay's
The Beggar's Opera, and Pope's *The Dunciad* – may have had
their provenance and inspiration in the meetings of this group.
For his services to the ministry Swift was made Dean of St
Patrick's Cathedral in Dublin in 1713, which was in the gift of
the Second Duke of Ormonde. Queen Anne, it appears, would
not countenance Swift's appointment to an English bishopric,
the preferment to which Swift aspired. With the death of

11

Queen Anne, collapse of the Tory government, and accession of the House of Hanover in 1714, Whig rule returned to England and Ireland. The political party and its leaders to which Swift had tied his fortunes were now proscribed men. Swift tried to keep a low profile in Ireland during the first years of what was for him a Hanoverian reign of terror. His literary labours were principally historical memoirs of the last four years of Queen Anne's reign. Swift saw himself as custodian of the Tory record. *Gulliver's Travels*, which he began writing in the early 1720s, would be a political–philosophical meditation on his experience at the centre of high politics as well as an intervention in more immediate political occasions.

Swift's first pamphlet on Ireland since becoming Dean of St Patrick's in 1713 and his first known political intervention since the Hanoverian accession was *A Proposal for the Universal Use of Irish Manufacture*, published in 1720 by the Tory printer Edward Waters, who was proceeded against for sedition. The work can be said to anticipate Sein Fein tactics in its economic proposals. In the pamphlet Swift mentions hearing 'a pleasant Observation of some Body's; *that* Ireland *would never be happy 'till a Law were made for* burning *every Thing that came from* England, *except their* People *and their* Coals' (PW ix. 17). An incendiary comment that would be appropriated by the IRA in the slogan: 'Burn everything English except their coal.' Between 1724 and 1725 Swift wrote seven pamphlets in the guise of a Dublin draper ('M. B. Drapier') opposing a patent granted to the English entrepreneur William Wood to manufacture copper coinage for Ireland. The incendiary flavour of these *Drapier's Letters* is suggested by the initials 'M.B.', which may stand for the tyrannicide 'Marcus Brutus'. King George I was Caesar in the *Drapier's Letters* (PW x. 21). These pamphlets powerfully fuelled Irish resistance to a measure seen as deleterious to the Irish economy and the result of corruption in the Hanoverian court (Wood had reputedly bribed the King's mistress, the Duchess of Kendal, for the patent). The famous fourth *Drapier's Letter* (printed on 22 October 1724) provocatively took the controversy into the radical territory of claiming Irish legislative independence from the Parliament in England. The rhetorical appeal of the pamphlet is radical 'To the whole People of IRELAND' (title page, PW x. 51, 53), but the pamphlet actually addresses the ethnically English, Protestant, and propertied people of Ireland (*PW* x. 55). The Whig government offered a reward of £300 for the author's identity. But Swift was not betrayed. A scriptural passage (1 Sam. 14: 45) was popularly invoked: 'And the people said . . . Shall Jonathan die, who hath wrought this great salvation in Israel? God forbid . . . So the people rescued Jonathan, that he died not.' Swift's most famous work, *Gulliver's Travels* (1726), was written during this period of Irish pamphleteering and activism. In the satiric ironic fantasy *A Modest Proposal* (1729) Swift once again advances the idea that the Irish should consume only what is made in Ireland. But with black humour the proposal is that the Irish should eat their babies. This pamphlet proposing a cannibal solution to the Irish problem is Swift's jeremiad against his people and is calculated to shock readers to attention and reflect on an Ireland *in extremis*. Swift's last pamphlet on Ireland was published in 1737. *A Proposal for Giving Badges to the Beggars*, unusually, was signed by Swift. The original title page identified the work as by the 'Dean of St Patrick's' and had an image of the Dean with 'M. B. Drapier' printed underneath. Swift acknowledged the work and invoked his full authority for it as Dean and Irish patriot. Swift's punitive severity against vagabond beggars (they deserve 'to be rooted out off the Face of the Earth') in this pamphlet should give pause to literary critics who suppose that the Houyhnhnms and their social policy in part IV of *Gulliver's Travels* are being condemned when they debate whether the Yahoos should be 'exterminated from the Face of the Earth' (*PW* xi. 271).

In the 1730s Swift produced some of his finest poetry, such as *Verses on the Death of Dr Swift, D.S.P.D.*, the so-called excremental or scatological poems ('The Lady's Dressing Room', 'A Beautiful Young Nymph Going to Bed', 'Strephon and Chloe', 'Cassinus and Peter'), 'To a Lady', 'On Poetry: A Rhapsody', and 'A Character, Panegyric, and Description of the Legion Club'. In a letter to John Gay and the Duchess of Queensberry of 28 August 1731 Swift wrote that he had

two great works in hand, one to reduce the whole politeness wit, humor & style of England into a short System for the use of all persons of quality, and particularly the Maids of Honor: The other is of almost equal importance; I may call it the whole duty of servants, in about twenty several Stations from the Steward & waiting woman down to the Scullion & Pantry boy. (*Corr.* iii. 493)

The first of these Swiftian projects was a satiric compilation, tending to the encyclopaedic, of endemic linguistic abuse in the Whig culture of politeness. *A Complete Collection of Genteel and Ingenious Conversation, According to the Most Polite Mode and Method Now Used at Court, and in the Best Companies of England. In Three Dialogues. By Simon Wagstaff, Esq.*, published in 1738, is the product of years of collecting. In this mechanical operation of conversation Swift records proverbs and colloquialisms, contemporary clichés, platitudes, slang, and word abuse. The other major satiric collection, *Directions to Servants*, remained unfinished and was published posthumously in 1745. He worked on his 'whole duty of servants' for many years. This compendium of the quotidian iniquities and manic turpitude of servants presents a master's nightmare of household subversion and anarchy. The 'Corruptions of Servants', violently inveighed against by Swift from the pulpit (see his sermon 'Causes of the Wretched Condition of Ireland', *PW* ix. 203–4), are on satiric display in *Directions to Servants*. An extract from this work begins the surrealist André Breton's *Anthologie de l'humour noir* (*Anthology of Black Humour*).[8] Swift became senile in his last years and was declared of unsound mind in 1742. He died in 1745 and is buried in St Patrick's Cathedral in Dublin. His famous epitaph in Latin contained in his will and later inscribed on 'a Black Marble' on the wall of St Patrick's Cathedral, presents Swift to after ages as the champion of human liberty (*PW* xiii. 149). The last likenesses of Swift are a series of profile portraits by the Irish artist Rupert Barber, son of Swift's friend the poet Mary Barber, and dated *c.* 1745. The fine Barber bust portrait of Swift in the collection of Bryn Mawr College has a symbolic ornamental frame. The sides are adorned with oak leaves and the corners of the frame have petalled Tudor roses. The oak leaf was a Tory emblem strongly associated with Stuart monarchy and offensive to the Hanoverians after 1714; the Tudor rose was an emblem of monarchy.[9] The image of Swift presented to posterity at the end of his life was of a champion of liberty and loyal adherent of Tory monarchy.

One fact of Swift's biography is of the first importance in understanding his career and writings. He was a High Church clergyman of the Church of Ireland. Swift declared that 'as to religion, I confessed myself to be an High-churchman, and that I did not conceive how any one, who wore the habit of a clergyman, could be otherwise' (*PW* viii. 120). Family memory of his paternal grandfather's sufferings in the cause of Charles I during and after the Civil Wars undoubtedly influenced Swift's perspective on the key contemporary political question of civil liberties. The memory of Swift's Cavalier grandfather is evoked in *A Letter from a Member of the House of Commons in Ireland to a Member of the House of Commons in England, concerning the Sacramental Test* (December 1708). Swift maintains in this pamphlet that the Test Act should never be repealed. Non-Anglican Protestants should either conform to the Established Church or be deprived of full civil rights, because, if once given power, the Protestant Dissenters, like the Puritans of old, would persecute members of the episcopal Church. Swift's Irish MP would 'be forced my self to keep a Chaplain disguised like my Butler, and steal to Prayers in a back Room, as my Grandfather used in those Times when the Church of *England* was *malignant*' (*PW* ii.121). Swift was a Tory conformist not a Whig tolerationist, and the publication of this pamphlet registers his ideological break from the English Whig Party, with which he had been associated in public and which sought to remove the Test for Protestant Dissenters in Ireland. The rabbling of the Scots episcopal clergy and the abolition of episcopacy in Scotland for which Swift blamed William III (*PW* v. 290) would only have reinforced his High Church resolve to preserve the rights, powers, and privileges of the Established Church in England and Ireland. When he was the 'Examiner', Swift would break with the politic Tory ministerial line he was supposed to be propounding in order to defend 'an *Episcopal Clergyman* of Scotland' and denounce the 'Tyranny' of his Presbyterian persecutors (*PW* iii.100–1).

Swift was militant in defence of Anglican orthodoxy, but the depth of his Christian belief was questioned in his own time and since. A Whig pamphleteer said Swift's 'Affection to the Church was never doubted, tho' his Christianity was ever question'd'. The anticlerical Whig, Anthony Collins, whose *Discourse of Freethinking* (1713) was parodied by Swift, said that Swift was made Dean of St Patrick's in Dublin under Queen Anne for his services as a High Church satirist against *'Whigs, Dissenters*, and the *War* with *France'*. Collins claimed that the Archbishop of York 'attempted to hinder his Promotion, by representing to her Majesty "What a Scandal it would be both to Church and State to bestow Preferment upon a Clergyman, who was hardly suspected of being a Christian" '. It was seen as part of a hack author's apprenticeship in the eighteenth century 'to libel Dean Swift for infidelity'.[10] Swift blamed Queen Anne and the Archbishop of York for blocking his ecclesiastical preferment in England on account of his authorship of *A Tale of a Tub* and poetic libels ('The Author upon Himself', ll. 1–6; *Poems*, 163). As a clergyman Swift regarded himself as being on combat duty: 'I look upon myself, in the capacity of a clergyman, to be one appointed by providence for defending a post assigned me, and for gaining over as many enemies as I can' (*PW* ix. 262). The enemies were theological, ecclesiological, and political. The principal theological enemies were the heterodox opponents of Trinitarian Anglican orthodoxy, such as the Socinians, and Enthusiasts, such as the Quakers. The Socinians are a principal target of Swift's *An Argument against Abolishing Christianity* (1708, first published 1711). The Quakers, 'the most absurd Heresy that ever appeared in the World' (*PW* vii. 107), are a specific target in the satire on Enthusiasm in section VIII of *A Tale of a Tub* and in *A Discourse concerning the Mechanical Operation of the Spirit* (1704). The ecclesiological enemies were the anticlerical opponents of the priesthood. High-profile anticlerical writers such as John Toland ('the great Oracle of the *Anti-Christians'*, *PW* ii. 37), Matthew Tindal (the Whig 'Apostle', *PW* iii. 39), and Anthony Collins (author of 'Atheology', *PW* iv. 27) appear in Swift's satiric pillory. The political enemies were monarchs, Whigs, and Low Churchmen prepared to make concessions to Protestant Dissenters from the Established Church. Swift's polemic and satire anathematize princes and parliaments perceived to be hostile to the rights, powers, and privileges of the Church as a spiritual corporation and to Anglican hegemony in the public life of Ireland and England. Swift demonized the Whig administration of 1708–10 and the post-1714 Hanoverian Whig regime in Ireland and England for attempting to undermine the status of the Established Church and the privileges of its clergy.

The contemporary Whig parliamentary attack on clerical privilege recalled for Swift the robbing of the Church at the Reformation by 'that Monster and Tyrant, Henry VIII. who took away from them, against law, reason, and justice, at least two thirds of their legal possessions' (*PW* xiii. 123). Swift's marginalia in a copy of Edward Herbert, Lord Cherbury's *The Life and Raigne of King Henry the Eighth* (1649) excoriates Henry VIII: 'And I wish he had been Flead, his skin stuffed and hangd on a Gibbet, His bulky guts and Flesh left to be devoured by Birds and Beasts for a warning to his Successors for ever. Amen.' (*PW* v. 251). Sir Thomas More, beheaded by Henry VIII, is a Swiftian hero, 'a person of the greatest virtue this kingdom ever produced', and martyr for the Church against tyranny (*PW* xiii, 123; v. 247, 248). In part III of *Gulliver's Travels*, More is the only modern figure mentioned in a '*Sextumvirate*' of the illustrious dead 'to which all the Ages of the World cannot add a Seventh' (*PW* xi. 196).

For Swift the great religious and political question of his day was whether liberty of conscience or conformity to the Established Church should prevail in public life. In a sermon 'On the Testimony of Conscience' he characteristically limits '*Liberty of Conscience*' to 'no more than a Liberty of knowing our own Thoughts; which Liberty no one can take from us'. He explains that the words have been abused and have acquired mistaken meanings:

> Liberty of Conscience is now-a-days not only understood to be the Liberty of believing what Men please, but also of endeavouring to propagate the Belief as much as they can, and to overthrow the Faith which the Laws have already established, to be rewarded by the Publick for those wicked Endeavours: And this is the Liberty of Conscience which the Fanaticks are now openly in the Face of the World endeavouring at with their utmost Application. (*PW* ix. 151)

17

This liberty of conscience 'produces revolutions, or at least convulsions and disturbances in a state' and for Swift the Civil Wars of the 1640s and the Revolution of 1688 were 'flaming instances' (*PW* ix. 263). A 'Fanatick Party' opposed to the apostolic institution of episcopal spiritual government had 'set all in a Flame' in the 1640s. Swift believed that it was 'in the Reign of King *Charles* I' that '*England* became, in a great Degree, a Protestant Kingdom ... But the *Puritans*, and other Schismaticks ... by an open Rebellion, destroyed that legal Reformation ... murdered their King, and changed the Monarchy into a Republick' (*PW* xii. 287, 289–90). Since the Revolution of 1688–9, Swift thought, 'men have sate much looser in the true fundamentals both of religion and government' and have taken up 'those very opinions professed by the leaders in that rebellion, which carried the blessed Martyr to the scaffold' (*PW* ix. 224). Swift supported coercive conformity to the established episcopal Church.[11] In *Gulliver's Travels* public conformity to the established religion is an ideal of good government (*PW* xi. 60, 131).

Significantly, Swift praised King Charles I and King Charles XII of Sweden, whom his Whig contemporaries regarded as arbitrary rulers of intolerant 'High Church' regimes. He praised the High Church Archbishop of Canterbury William Sancroft, who stood firm against King James II's attempt to impose liberty of conscience by prerogative edict in 1687–8 and who was driven out of his see by William III after the Revolution in 1691. Swift bitterly opposed Whig parliamentary attempts to repeal the Sacramental Test Act. This Act was designed to protect Anglican hegemony by requiring communion in the Church of England as a qualification for public office. Whig money behind an attempt to repeal the Test in 1733 he despaired 'is sufficient among us – to abolish Christianity it self' (*Corr.* iv. 211). Many of Swift's tracts relating to Ireland are defences of the exclusive position of the Established Church and privileges of its clergy against hostile parliaments. Swift wrote on behalf of Ireland against English oppression, but the Irish patriot was also a High Churchman. When James Butler, the Second Duke of Ormonde, a High Church Tory, is Lord Lieutenant of Ireland (1703–7 and 1710–13), Swift makes no public complaint about England's treatment of Ireland. But he erupts into print against English Whig administrations perceived to be sympathetic to the claims of Protestant Dissenters for relief from persecution by statute or otherwise ruining Ireland for the advantage of private interests in England.

Modern readings of Swift are apt to underestimate just how much his political vision was refracted by his Carolinist and High Church religious allegiance. Swift venerated his paternal grandfather, the Royalist vicar, 'for his extraordinary Services and zeal, and persecutions in the royal cause' and commemorated him with a monument (*PW* v. 190, 334). His autobiographical fragment 'Family of Swift' and marginalia in a copy of Clarendon's *History of the Rebellion* – which Swift read four times – indicate his identification with his grandfather's cause (see *PW* v. 187–95; 295–320). In 1726, the year that *Gulliver's Travels* was first published, Swift preached 'A Sermon upon the Martyrdom of K. Charles I'. He describes Charles I as 'that excellent King and blessed Martyr . . . who rather chose to die on a scaffold than betray the religion and liberties of his people, wherewith GOD and the laws had entrusted him' (*PW* ix. 219). Swift's famous declaration of his own commitment to liberty in *Verses on the Death of Dr Swift, D.S.P.D.* ('Fair LIBERTY was all his cry; | For her he stood prepared to die') echoes a passage in John Denham's Royalist poem *Coopers Hill* alluding to the trial and martyrdom of Charles I ('Fair liberty pursu'd, and meant a Prey | To lawless power, here turn'd, and stood at bay').[12] Swift was a Carolinist clergyman whose major satires are politically oriented by High Church partisanship. In the violent imaginary of this High Churchman's satire there are individual satiric killings and calls to massacre.

The late-seventeenth-century English satirist Tom Brown, in *A Short Essay on English Satire*, wrote conventionally that 'Satire is design'd to expose Vice and encourage Vertue'. Daniel Defoe wrote that the 'end of Satyr is reformation'.[13] Swift subscribed to the satirist's conventional moral brief with varying degrees of irony. An apology for his satiric art is offered in his ironic poetic obituary for himself, *Verses on the Death of Dr Swift* (1739):

19

> Yet, malice never was his aim;
> He lashed the vice but spared the name.
> . . . .
> His satire points at no defect,
> But what all mortals may correct
>
> (ll. 463–4, 467–8; *Poems*, 497)

This declaration of moral purpose and disavowal of personal malice are highly suspect and problematic. This very poem is full of named victims, and a powerful effect of Swiftian satire with its dissected beaux and dismembered nymphs is that the human carcase is radically defective and humankind too depraved to save. Swift's violent personal satire often seems aimed at erasing rather than reforming its subject, as in the execution of his mock-astrological hoax on John Partridge or in the invective satire against William Wood in *The Drapier's Letters*, and in poems such as 'Wood, an Insect' which concludes:

> But now, since the Drapier hath heartily mauled him,
> I think the best thing we can do is to scald him.
> For which operation there's nothing more proper
> Than the liquor he deals in, his own melted copper;
> Unless, like the Dutch, you rather would boil
> This coiner of raps in a cauldron of oil.
> Then choose which you please, and let each bring a faggot,
> For our fear's at an end with the death of the maggot.
>
> (*Poems*, 288)

Poems such as 'Traulus' (*Poems*, 422–7) and 'A Character, Panegyric, and Description of the Legion Club' (*Poems*, 550–6), for example, are violently punitive, aimed at the condemnation not correction of their subjects. In several places, famously in the fourth part of *Gulliver's Travels*, where the Houyhnhnms debate whether the humanoid Yahoos 'should be exterminated from the Face of the Earth' (*PW* xi. 271), Swift's punitive fury expresses itself in echoes of God's words in Genesis 6: 7 in the King James Authorized Version. The Old Testament Book and particularly the story of the Flood are an important presence in Swift's satiric utterance and punitive satiric project against humankind.[14] 'Drown the World', Swift wrote to Alexander Pope on 26 November 1725, 'I am not content with despising it, but I would anger it if I could with safety' (*Corr.* iii. 117). He is not, in this famous letter on the intentions behind *Gulliver's Travels*, expressing interest in changing or reforming the world. A village pump version of the Flood that will destroy humankind from the face of the earth is threatened in 'Baucis and Philemon' (ll. 46–8, *Poems*, 103). In a mock-scaffold speech entitled *The Last Speech and Dying Words of Ebenezor Elliston*, printed at the time of the condemned felon's execution in 1722, Swift has Elliston say that the government should have hanged him long ago. The condemned crook says: 'we ought to be looked upon as the common Enemies of Mankind; whose Interest it is to root us out like Wolves, and other mischievous Vermin, against which no fair Play is required' (*PW* ix. 41). Under his own signature Swift advances a 'very plain Proposal' to badge Irish beggars and writes that vagabond beggars are fit 'to be rooted out off the Face of the Earth' (*PW* xiii. 132, 139). An earlier 'Modest Proposal' to remove the burden of the improvident Irish poor with a cannibal scheme is the ironic, satiric fantasy version of this punitive animus that expresses itself in calls to massacre.

Swift's satires were first published anonymously or pseudonymously and deploy putative speakers. Swift preferred impersonation to speaking *in propria persona*, as Alexander Pope's famous tribute to Swift in *The Dunciad* celebrates. It is a characteristic of his satire. A combination of reasons explains this predilection. Personal safety was undoubtedly uppermost. Swift's works do often have scandalous, seditious, subversive, and indeed treasonous elements, often unrecognized by modern readers, but attested to by clouds of contemporary witnesses. The man was also guarded temperamentally. His ubiquitous use of irony and indirection and refusal of plain statement reflect this constitutional cautiousness. Obviously, too, anonymous and pseudonymous publication allowed Swift the freedom to infiltrate his texts unnoticed. There was also the residual feeling in the eighteenth century, and Swift shared the ethos, that it was unbecoming for gentlemen to appear under their own name in the press. Swift also clearly enjoyed the mystification of anonymity and pseudonymity. As he says in the anonymous 'Apology' for *A Tale of a Tub*, the reception of the work among men of wit has been such as '*to give him the vanity of telling his Name, wherein the World with all its wise*

21

Conjectures, is yet very much in the dark, which Circumstance is no disagreeable Amusement either to the Publick or himself (PW i. 11).

It needs to be frankly confronted that the radical project of much Swiftian satire is misanthropic. In the words of the putative author of *A Tale of a Tub*, the 'Carcass of *Humane Nature*' is dissected in Swift's satiric anatomies and left exposed 'till at last it *smelt* so strong' that it can be preserved no longer (*PW* i. 77). Swiftian satire attempts to persuade readers that men and women are utterly corrupt and fit only for extermination from the face of the earth. The satiric project is undoubtedly informed by an Augustinian conviction of fallen human nature. The typical strategy of Swift's misanthropic satire is to identify some pariah group and then conflate all men and women with the despised group.[15] In part IV of *Gulliver's Travels* the Yahoos are identified as barbaric and bestial and the satire works to conflate human with Yahoo. In *A Tale of a Tub* the common London spectacle of a specific class of woman, the female felon or prostitute, being carted and whipped, becomes a 'Woman *flay'd*' in Swift's satire (*PW* i. 109). Neither is the violence just directed against the female body. The male carcass is cut up also:

> Last Week I saw a Woman *flay'd*, and you will hardly believe, how much it altered her Person for the worse. Yesterday I ordered the Carcass of a *Beau* to be stript in my Presence; when we were all amazed to find so many unsuspected Faults under one Suit of Cloaths: Then I laid open his *Brain*, his *Heart*, and his *Spleen*; But, I plainly perceived at every Operation, that the farther we proceeded, we found the Defects encrease upon us in Number and Bulk . . .   (*PW* i. 109–10)[16]

By impudent contrast, when Swift performs an autopsy on himself in his ironic obituary *Verses on the Death of Dr Swift*, the doctors report: 'when we opened him we found, | That all his vital parts were sound' (ll. 175–6, *Poems*, 490).

Swift was aware of the quixotic nature of a satiric enterprise against humankind and reflected on its ultimate impotence. In 'The Preface' to *A Tale of a Tub* it is explained that general and misanthropic satire is innocuous:

> Satyr being levelled at all, is never resented for an offence by any, since every individual Person makes bold to understand it of

22

others, and very wisely removes his particular Part of the Burthen upon the shoulders of the World, which are broad enough, and able to bear it . . . you may securely display your utmost *Rhetorick* against Mankind, in the Face of the World; tell them, *'That all are gone astray; That there is none that doth good, no not one; That we live in the very Dregs of Time; That Knavery and Atheism are Epidemick as the Pox; That Honesty is fled with Astraea'*; with any other Common places *equally* new and eloquent . . . And when you have done, the whole Audience, far from being offended, shall return you thanks as a Deliverer of precious and useful Truths . . . 'Tis but a *Ball* bandied to and fro, and every Man carries a *Racket* about Him to strike it from himself among the rest of the Company. (*PW* i. 31)

Declaration of the ineffectiveness of general or disguised personal satire was a routine rebuke of readers among hard-core, hardline satirists, which Swift here parodies and repli-cates. Joseph Hall, for example, in *Virgidemiarum* (1598–9), a work esteemed by Alexander Pope as 'the best poetry and truest satire in the English language', writes: 'Who list com-plaine of wronged faith or fame | When hee may shift it to anothers name.'[17]

'The Preface of the Author' in *The Battle of the Books* states:

SATYR *is a sort of* Glass, *wherein Beholders do generally discover every body's Face but their Own; which is the chief Reason for that kind of Reception it meets in the World, and that so very few are offended with it. But if it should happen otherwise, the Danger is not great; and, I have learned from long Experience, never to apprehend Mischief from those Understandings, I have been able to provoke; For, Anger and Fury, though they add Strength to the* Sinews *of the* Body, *yet are found to relax those of the* Mind, *and to render all its Efforts feeble and impotent.* (PW i. 140)

In satirizing general satire as impotent, because it misses its target, Swift also coyly indicates that his satire can sting. It is the hapless, infuriated victims who are said to be incapable of hurting the satirist. This passage in 'The Preface of the Author', satirizing the futility of general satire due to the insensibility of readers, is in fact personal satire: a precise, specific ridicule of a cultural broker of the Whig elite, John Vanbrugh. In his early poems, 'The History of Vanbrug's House' (dated 1706, *Poems*, 91–2) and 'Vanbrug's House' (draft dated 1703, *Poems*, 96–9), Swift satirized Vanbrugh, the Whig dramatist and architect, member of the elite Whig Kit-Cat Club, and a high-profile figure in the new Whig culture of moneyed men, as the epitome of the Modern, his pretension to architectural grandeur mocked by his contemptible, small-scale achievement. Swift's satire hit its target, incensing Vanbrugh (*PW* xv. 83–4). The sardonic commentary on modern architecture in each part of *Gulliver's Travels* is a reprise of Swift's personal satiric ridicule of the Whig architect.[18] In this 'Preface' to *The Battle of the Books* Swift mocks as trite and facile Vanbrugh's claims for his dramatic satire made in the anticlerical 'Prologue' to his major play *The Provoked Wife* (1697). Vanbrugh had written:

> Since 'tis the intent and business of the stage
> To copy out the follies of the age,
> To hold to every man a faithful glass
> And show him of what species he's an ass,
>
> .   .   .   .   .   .
>
> And that the satire may be sure to bite
> Kind heaven inspire some venomed priest to write . . .[19]

The venomed priest pointed out that Vanbrugh was the ass in the mirror for thinking his satire could bite.

In 'A Letter from Capt. Gulliver, to his Cousin Sympson', which prefaces the 1735 edition of the *Travels*, Swift also mocks the satiric project of reforming the world. The proud, ranting recluse in his little garden at Redriff has absurd expectations of reformation, which his misanthropic conviction (endorsed by Swift's radical satire) should not have allowed him to entertain. Gulliver complains to his cousin that he should never have published his *Travels*:

> Pray bring to your Mind how often I desired you to consider, when you insisted on the Motive of *publick Good*; that the *Yahoos* were a Species of Animals utterly incapable of Amendment by Precepts or Examples: And so it hath proved; for instead of seeing a full Stop put to all Abuses and Corruptions, at least in this little Island, as I had Reason to expect: Behold, after above six Months Warning, I cannot learn that my Book hath produced one single Effect according to mine Intentions.

He concludes: 'I should never have attempted so absurd a Project as that of reforming the *Yahoo* Race in this Kingdom;

but, I have now done with all such visionary Schemes for ever' (*PW* xi. 6, 8).

The reading public's anticipated insensibility to satire only renewed Swift's efforts to shock it to attention. The admission of the futility of satire faced with flagitious humankind – satire's inability to produce shame – is often part of the mordant satiric effect in Swift. An astringent personal satire on the anticlerical Whig Lord Lieutenant of Ireland, Thomas, Earl of Wharton ('He is a Presbyterian in Politics, and an Atheist in Religion; but he chuseth at present to whore with a Papist') is prefaced with the observation that Wharton 'is without the Sense of Shame or Glory, as some Men are without the Sense of Smelling; and, therefore, a good Name to him is no more than a precious Ointment would be to these' (*PW* iii. 179, 178). The satirist is sure he cannot harm the Earl of Wharton:

> when these Papers are public, it is Odds but he will tell me, as he once did upon a like Occasion, that he is damnably mauled; and then with the easiest Transition in the World, ask about the Weather, or the Time of the Day? So that I enter on the Work with more Chearfulness, because I am sure, neither to make him angry, nor any Way hurt his Reputation; a Pitch of Happiness and Security to which his Excellency hath arrived, which no Philosopher before him could reach. (*PW* iii. 178)

In the famous letter to Alexander Pope of 29 September 1725 on the intention behind *Gulliver's Travels*, Swift wrote that 'the chief end I propose to my self in all my labors is to vex the world rather then divert it, and if I could compass that designe without hurting my own person or Fortune I would be the most Indefatigable writer you have ever seen' (*Corr.* iii. 102). Pseudonymous or anonymous publication, ironic obliquity, and innuendo rather than explicit statement were some of the means by which Swift sought to compass his design in safety. Gulliver, who tells the reader that his 'principal design was to inform, and not to amuse thee', is the putative author who delivers the misanthropic verdicts. Formally it is Gulliver who is to be charged with blasphemy and madness, not the Anglican Dean. Also, the artful generality of satires such as *Gulliver's Travels* as published enabled Swift (and his printer) to evade prosecution. However, Swiftian general satire should

25

be understood as convenient shorthand for the many victims who could be named; a summary saturation bombing of the group rather than case-by-case capital punishment.[20] In *Verses on the Death of Dr Swift* it is said of Swift's general satire on vice: 'No individual could resent, | Where thousands equally were meant' (ll. 465–6, *Poems*, 497). Swift's general satire more than glances at particular cases: it is generated by them: 'In describing the Virtues and Vices of Mankind, it is convenient, upon every Article, to have some eminent Person in our Eye, from whence we copy our Description' (*PW* iii. 10–11). My account of Swift's satiric works will indicate some of their particular, topical targets.

In reaction to criticism in the eighteenth and nineteenth centuries that recoiled from Swift in disgust, literary criticism in the twentieth century recuperated Swift's writing for modern readers. Interpretations were produced in which, for example, the apparent misanthropy of *Gulliver's Travels* was sanitized and its seditious menaces occluded. The High Churchman whose polemical extremism was feared by contemporary Whig authorities has had an afterlife as a moderate with progressive and secularist political views. Like John Middleton Murry's earlier 'Writers and their Work' study, this book sees Swift as a dangerous writer. But Swift's signature extremism is explained here in terms of ideology and cultural context rather than personal pathology.

2

⸻⸻⸻⸻⸻⸻⸻⸻⸻⸻⸻⸻

A Tale of a Tub

A Tale of a Tub, the scandalous and brilliant prose satire of Swift's early career, was probably begun in the mid-1690s, when he was a parish priest in Kilroot, County Antrim, an Anglican outpost in a Presbyterian region. He completed it in England, while working for Sir William Temple at Moor Park. The book containing *A Tale of a Tub*, *The Battle of the Books*, and *A Discourse concerning the Mechanical Operation of the Spirit* was published anonymously in 1704. Swift's authorial intention in *A Tale of a Tub* is explained in the 'Apology' affixed to the enlarged fifth edition of 1710. This prose satire is aimed at *'the numerous and gross Corruptions in Religion and Learning'*. The *'Abuses in Religion he proposed to set forth in the Allegory of the Coats, and the three Brothers, which was to make up the Body of the Discourse. Those in Learning he chose to introduce by way of Digressions'* (*PW* i. 1). Many years later Swift echoed this apologetic for his satire in the *Intelligencer*, no. III (1728): 'although some Things are too serious, solemn, or sacred to be turned into Ridicule, yet the Abuses of them are certainly not; since it is allowed, that Corruptions in *Religion* ... may be proper *Topicks* ... of *Satyr*' (*PW* xii. 33). The satire on the 'Abuses' in religion is directed at Roman Catholicism, Protestant Dissent, and sectarian Enthusiasm and is conducted principally in sections II, IV, VI, VIII, XI, and in the *Discourse concerning the Mechanical Operation of the Spirit*.

The satire's religious positive is what the Anglican Church, reformed from popery, claimed to be – that is, a Catholic and Apostolic church adhering to Scripture and the practice of the Primitive Church in the first centuries after Christ. Swift's parable of the Father (God) who gives his three sons a Will (the

27

New Testament) that contains full instructions in the wearing and caring of their Coats (Christian Faith and Doctrine) places particular importance on uniformity and speaks euphemistically of preventing schism and killing heretics. In the beginning the sons 'carefully observed their Father's Will, and kept their Coats in very good Order . . . they travelled thro' several Countries, encountred a reasonable Quantity of Gyants and slew certain Dragons' (*PW* i. 44–5). The rest of the *Tale* explores the degeneration from this 'good Order', drawing on the vast arsenal of Anglican apologetic and controversial writing to deride Roman Catholicism and Protestant Dissent. Peter (popery) corrupts his coat with self-serving accretions and Jack (Dissent) tears his coat during his reformation from Peter. Martin (who embodies the moderate Reformation of Luther and later the Anglican via media) manages to restore his coat without destroying the basic fabric. Swift's satire increasingly focuses on Jack's violent career of iconoclasm and schism, leaving little doubt as to where Swift thinks the greatest threat lies to the Church and State. Two of Swift's non-fictional prose works, the posthumously published violent sermon on *Brotherly Love* (*PW* ix. 169–79) and the unfinished 'Concerning that Universal Hatred, which Prevails against the Clergy' (*PW* xiii. 123–6), afford the modern reader with interesting glosses on the religious allegory of the *Tale* and indicate that Swift regarded Jack (Protestant Dissent) as the greater contemporary civil and religious threat.

The continuous narrative in the *Tale* allegorizing corruptions in religion is disrupted by Digressions in which 'Modernist' corruptions in learning are satirized. In the Digressions and in *The Battle of the Books* Swift intervenes on the side of the 'Ancients' in an old and continuing paper war over the claims of Ancient and Modern culture. As an object, *A Tale of a Tub* presents itself as an artefact of modern print culture. It is a satiric parody of abuses in the printed book. There is an elaborate array of paratexts. The reader first negotiates a title page, list of forthcoming publications, Apology, Postscript, Dedication to Lord Somers, Dedication to Posterity, Preface, and Introduction before the Tale proper begins. The narrative is immediately interrupted by a digression. The putative author of the *Tale*, an enthusiast for all things heretical and insane, is a protean hack from the world of Grub Street. In the 'Apology' the real author claims *'that through the whole Book he has not borrowed one single Hint from any Writer in the World'* (*PW* i. 6). The putative author declares his originality on the title page, derivatively, by a quotation from Lucretius, himself a highly appropriative writer. Swift's satire is radically parodic and ironic. The text is a display of allusive recurrence. The High Church Tory Francis Atterbury rightly remarked in 1704 that the book was 'an original in it's [*sic*] kind'.[1] But it does belong to a literary kind. In its paratextual play, learned wit, and pathologizing of puritanism, *A Tale of a Tub* has some kinship with the great textual assemblage in Swift's Anglican literary culture, Robert Burton's cento *The Anatomy of Melancholy* (1621–38), a work from which Swift borrowed. *A Tale of a Tub*, a richly intertextual work, is really a satiric cento.

The satire on abuses in religion has a contextual location in contemporary Anglican pamphleteering: in anti-popery, anti-Puritan satire, anti-Quaker propaganda, and in Church of England polemical responses to anticlericalism. Its ideological bite derives from the period 1687–1704. This work is a high-cultural product of the Anglican paper war against James II's prerogative toleration of Roman Catholics and Protestant Nonconformists in 1687–8 and of the Anglican reaction to heterodoxy and Dissent after the passing of the Toleration Act in 1689. The satire on modern learning in the work identifies it with the 'Ancient' stance adopted by Swift's first patron Sir William Temple and by the Tory wits of Christ Church Oxford, against William Wotton and Richard Bentley, in a recent English outbreak of the Ancients and Moderns controversy. The work was a High Churchman's reaction to the Church of England's enemies and an ideological conservative's reaction to modernity. Imaginatively, however, it is utterly unconventional, the work of a radical and a postmodernist.

As Swift's 'Apology' makes plain, *A Tale of a Tub* was mistaken for the abuse it attacks. Even admirers of the book, like Francis Atterbury, considered the work to be profane in parts and dangerous for the author to acknowledge.[2] Certainly, in places the religious satire would appear to deride Jesus Christ as well as the infidels and radical Protestant Enthusiasts that are its ostensible target. In satirizing the Prophet of Islam, and radical Quaker prophets such as James Nayler (who rode into Bristol in 1656 on a donkey and who was prosecuted for blasphemy), Swift's text does not obviously except Jesus Christ who entered Jerusalem 'sitting upon an ass' (Matt. 21: 4–5):

> TIS recorded of *Mahomet*, that upon a Visit he was going to pay in *Paradise*, he had an Offer of several Vehicles to conduct him upwards . . . but he refused them all, and would be born to Heaven upon nothing but his *Ass*. Now, this Inclination of *Mahomet*, as singular as it seems, hath been since taken up by a great Number of devout *Christians*.   (*PW* i. 172)

The putative author, in order 'to avoid giving Offence to any Party', allegorizes the '*Ass*' as '*Gifted*, or *enlightened Teacher*' and '*Rider*' as '*Fanatick Auditory*' (*PW* i. 173). Similarly, in section IX of the *Tale*, 'A Digression concerning Madness', the propagation of new religions is diagnosed as '*Madness*': 'the Parent of all those mighty Revolutions, that have happened in *Empire*, in *Philosophy*, and in *Religion*. For, the Brain, in its natural Position and State of Serenity, disposeth its Owner to pass his Life in the common Forms, without any Thought of subduing Multitudes to his own *Power*, his *Reasons* or his *Visions*' (*PW* i. 108). This satiric pathology would not obviously except Jesus Christ.

Contemporaries pointed to several profane passages in the work. One of the more dangerous imputations was that the satire flirted with anti-Trinitarianism. In the 'Introduction' of *A Tale of a Tub* the hack author imitates 'that prudent Method observed by many other Philosophers and great Clerks, whose chief Art in Division has been, to grow fond of some proper mystical Number, which their Imaginations have rendred Sacred . . . Now among all the rest, the profound Number THREE is that which hath most employ'd my sublimest Speculations' (*PW* i. 34–5). 'A *Panegyrical Essay upon the Number* THREE' is promised and appears in the mock-list of forthcoming publications at the front of the book. The idea that the number three has magical properties was ancient. As Swift's protégé William Diaper wrote in the tenth of his *Nereides: or, Sea-Eclogues* (1712), recalling the stress on the number three in Virgil's eighth *Eclogue*: '(strange Vertues have been found | In Numbers hid; and Energy divine, | In figur'd Spells, and the mysterious Trine).'[3] Swift in this passage in the 'Introduction' of the *Tale* was ridiculing cabbalism. In the 'Apology' he defends himself from the charge of anti-Trinitarianism by claiming that he had written 'Four' in *'the Original Manuscript'*. The unauthorized change to *'the Number* Three' had led some to endeavour *'to squeeze out a dangerous Meaning that was never thought on. And indeed the Conceit was half spoiled by changing the Numbers; that of* Four *being much more Cabalistick, and therefore better exposing the pretended Virtue of Numbers, a Superstition there intended to be ridicul'd'* (*PW* i. 4). Indeed, the number four does have profound significance in the Qabalah, as the Four Letters of Tetragrammaton, the sacred name for God, which in Hebrew is spelt YHVH. Nevertheless, readers in Swift's time and since have felt that the freewheeling satire on corruptions does damage to the orthodox positions it claims to defend.

The 'Preface' of the Tale explains that only personal satire has impact in modern England (*PW* i. 31–2). Swift's general satire on *'Corruptions in Religion and Learning'* was certainly given needling specificity by having some high-profile contemporary figures as embodiments of the 'Abuses' in religion and culture. The modern Whig intellectual trinity of the classical scholars Richard Bentley and William Wotton, and the scientist, mathematician, and alchemist Isaac Newton are mercilessly ridiculed by name and through reductive burlesque of their ideas.[4] The representative Moderns (and Newtonians) Bentley and Wotton, satirized throughout the volume, are finally literally skewered together in the *Battle of the Books* (*PW* i. 164–5). Swift's satiric ridicule of modern learning and science as mechanistic in method and theory but really driven by irrational occult and mystical interests is acute satire of Isaac Newton, whose mechanical thinking in his published writings was influenced by alchemy. It was also said of Newton, who became Warden of the Mint in 1696, that he would be the first Whig hanged at a Jacobite restoration. Newton was notorious for prosecuting coiners under the treason statutes. Swift alludes to his violent activities at the Mint when he traces the criminal provenance of the word 'banter' used by Wotton in his critique of *A Tale of a Tub* to White-Friars, an underworld area where coiners operated: *'This Polite Word of theirs was first borrowed from the Bullies in* White-Fryars, *then fell among the Footmen, and at last retired to the Pedants, by whom it is applied as properly to the Productions of Wit, as if I should apply it to Sir* Isaac Newton's *Mathematicks' (PW* i. 10).[5] In 1696, the year when *A Tale of a Tub* is said to have been written and the year of the Jacobite Assassination Plot against William III, Swift's satire, as we have seen, apparently approves the assassination of another militaristic monarch (Henri IV). The King's mad militarism, cured by the assassin 'state-surgeon', is explained by a theory of attraction and vapours in what is recognizably a parody of Newtonian science *(PW* i. 103).[6] If 'Henri IV' is code for William III, as I have suggested, then it is black humour to have the fanatically anti-Jacobite Whig scientist supplying the theoretical justification for unspeakable operations actually projected by Jacobites in 1696. It is indicative of Swift's extremism that he never seems to have condemned the Assassination Plot against William III when he might have done so (indeed, rather, he later excoriated the man who betrayed the Jacobite Assassination Plot).[7]

But among the many victims of *A Tale of a Tub* and *The Battle of the Books* it is John Dryden who figures prominently and the reasons for the satiric parody of him are central to the book's satiric project.[8] Swift's satiric volume belatedly replies to Dryden's *The Hind and the Panther* (1687), a poem in which Dryden was understood to be supporting James II's policy of prerogative toleration of Roman Catholics and Protestant Dissenters in 1687–8. The satire represents the toleration of 1687–8 as a sinister conspiracy. In *A Tale of a Tub* Peter and Jack are said to have colluded in a design to trepan the Anglican brother Martin and the satire imputes 'a close Analogy' between Papists and Dissenters *(PW* i. 127–8, 131). The ridicule of the Roman Catholic convert's great poem in contemporary Anglican polemic is incorporated into the texture of Swift's satire. For instance, in one of these pamphlet attacks, Tom Brown's *The Late Converts Exposed*, Dryden's use of the quotation from Virgil in the epigraph on the title page of *The Hind and the Panther* ('Antiquam exquirite matrem' (seek your ancient mother)) is mocked and the convert is ridiculed as an obsessed genealogist.[9] Swift appropriated this contemporary caricature of Dryden in *The Battle of the Books*, puncturing Dryden's pretensions as the modern Virgil. In *The Battle* Dryden seeks out Virgil, claiming kinship: '*Dryden* in a long

Harangue soothed up the good *Antient*, called him *Father*, and by a large deduction of Genealogies, made it plainly appear, that they were nearly related' (*PW* i. 157). In Swift's satire Dryden's claim to be the modern Virgil is spurious.

For a High Churchman like Swift, Dryden was obnoxious as a prominent apostate. Dryden's Roman Catholic poem *The Hind and the Panther*, which provocatively welcomed James II's 'Declaration for Liberty of Conscience' in its address 'To the Reader' and in the poem proper, was his unforgivable work.[10] It is explicitly ridiculed as 'the Master-piece of a famous Writer now living, intended for a compleat Abstract of sixteen thousand Schoolmen from *Scotus* to *Bellarmin*' (*PW* i. 41). Swift's satire rewrites Dryden's claims for the Catholic Church made in the poem. In Dryden's allegorical poem the undivided Catholic Church alone defeats heretics, 'the Gyant-brood'. The 'dying Saviour's' 'will' is only rightly interpreted by the Catholic Church.[11] In *A Tale of a Tub* the future Protestant brothers are also confronting 'a reasonable Quantity of Gyants' and the Roman Catholic brother Peter is a confidence trickster, a modern literary critic who wrests the Father's 'Will' for his own ends.

Dryden also symbolizes modern literary decadence in *A Tale of a Tub*. A Dryden production is imputed to be principally about self-promotion. Swift's book is a hostile mimicry of the pathologically confessional paratextual display said to be characteristic of Dryden:

> *Prefaces, Epistles, Advertisements, Introductions, Prolegomena's, Apparatus's, To-the-Reader's*. This Expedient was admirable at first; Our Great *Dryden* has long carried it as far as it would go, and with incredible Success. He has often said to me in Confidence, that the World would have never suspected him to be so great a Poet, if he had not assured them so frequently in his Prefaces, that it was impossible they could either doubt or forget it. (*PW* i. 81–2)

Dryden is recognized as a celebrity, but his canonical status is insinuated to be insecure. The folio first edition of Dryden's translation of Virgil was sold unbound with do-it-yourself instructions for binding the several parts of the book.[12] The putative author of the *Tale* informs readers about an almost-instant remainder: 'there is now actually in being, a certain

Poet called *John Dryden*, whose Translation of *Virgil* was lately printed in a large Folio, well bound, and if diligent search were made, for ought I know, is yet to be seen' (*PW* i. 22). The hack author's book is as 'well bound' as Dryden's. At the end of section VII, 'A Digression in Praise of Digressions', the reader is invited to rearrange the section: 'I have chosen for it as proper a Place as I could readily find. If the judicious Reader can assign a fitter, I do here empower him to remove it into any other Corner he please' (*PW* i. 94). Swift's satire of the publishing event and appearance of Dryden's Virgil was proleptic of the actual empowerment of the reader that would come to pass in modern fiction and criticism. B. S. Johnson's famous 'book in a box', *The Unfortunates*, published in 1969, presented its twenty-seven sections unbound with the following direction: 'If readers prefer not to accept the random order in which they receive the novel, then they may re-arrange the sections into any other random order before reading.' The arbitrary linear sequence of the bound printed book is easily broken and rearranged in the age of the computer and hypertext. The chapters in the deconstructionist critic J. Hillis Miller's *Topographies* (1995), for instance, were not created in linear sequence and 'can easily be arranged in different orders'. 'The order of the chapters in the printed version is a somewhat arbitrary sequence that signals certain relations but hides others.'[13]

Swift and Dryden were related. They were second cousins, once removed, and there is an apocryphal hearsay story that Swift may have had a personal grudge against Dryden, who was supposed to have disparaged Swift's early pindaric odes. But Dryden's appearance in Swift's satiric volume can certainly be explained in ideological terms, and the pillorying of Dryden and other high-profile figures shows that Swift's general satire on religious and cultural corruption always has a personal or particular edge. He lashed what he saw as the vice but did not spare the name.

3

Shorter Satiric Works

SATIRIST AS ASSASSIN: 'THE BICKERSTAFF PAPERS'

The body count from Swift's satiric canon includes that of the leading contemporary London astrologer and almanac-maker John Partridge. A post-mortem on Swift's famous literary hoax killing of Partridge can disclose much about Swiftian satiric execution: its astringent ironic humour, cold-blooded intensity, attention to detail, summary justice, and ideological motive. Characteristically, Swift conceals his identity and impersonates the enemy – the High Church priest becomes an astrologer. Partridge was in the dark for a long time about the true identity of the assassin astrologer.

Partridge's high-profile almanac, *Merlinus Liberatus*, repeatedly challenged rival astrologers to draw up nativities and predict when people will die. His 'Monthly Observations' in his almanac for 1708 predicted a 'Distemper' possibly proving to be 'a Malignant Fever' in London in April. The astrologer observed for October that: 'Scribling and Lying are become Faculties of Profit and Credit; yet some of those Virtuosi are catcht and rewarded.'[1] Impersonating a rival astrologer, the fictional Isaac Bickerstaff Esq, Swift took up the challenge and delivered on Partridge's prognostications, publishing his own *Predictions for the Year 1708. Wherein the Month and Day of the Month are set down, the Persons named, and the great Actions and Events of next Year particularly related, as they will come to pass. Written to prevent the People of England from being further impos'd on by vulgar Almanack-makers. By Isaac Bickerstaff Esq.*[2] The *Predictions* begins with a nativity that is assumed to be almost beneath notice:

MY first Prediction is but a Trifle; yet I will mention it, to shew how ignorant those sottish Pretenders to Astrology are in their own Concerns: It relates to *Partrige* the Almanack-Maker; I have consulted the Star of his Nativity by my own Rules; and find he will infallibly die upon the 29th of *March* next, about eleven at Night, of a raging Fever: Therefore I advise him to consider of it, and settle his Affairs in Time.   (*PW* ii. 145)

A pamphlet entitled *Mr Partridge's Answer to Esquire Bicker-staff's Strange and Wonderful Predictions for the Year 1708* claimed Partridge was being menaced and that his life was in danger, but that he would be alive at the end of March to expose Bickerstaff's deceit. Bickerstaff's predictions were assessed as the work of a Jacobite (*PW* ii. 201, 204, 206, 207).

After 29 March, Swift brought out the sequel, completing a brilliant April Fool's Day hoax: *The Accomplishment of the First of Mr Bickerstaff's Predictions. Being an Account of the Death of Mr Partrige, the Almanack-maker, Upon the 29th Instant. In a Letter to a Person of Honour.* Swift now impersonates a grave, judicious gentleman author who reports that Partridge became ill and died as predicted by Isaac Bickerstaff. In Partridge's case there is doubt about when the clinical signs of raving began: 'The People about him said, he had been for some Hours delirious; but when I saw him, he had his Understanding as well as ever I knew.' The dying Partridge admits that Bickerstaff's predic-tion so affected him that it was the cause of his 'Distemper'. Asked why he did not cast his own nativity to see if Bickerstaff's prediction was accurate, Partridge, who confesses that astrology is an imposture, 'shook his Head, and said, O! Sir, this is no Time for jesting, but for repenting those Fooleries, as I do now from the very Bottom of my Heart' (*PW* ii. 154). In his almanac for 1709, the real Partridge replied that 'I am still alive' and was alive on the '29th of *March*' (*PW* ii. 225). In private Partridge reassured friends that he was well and speculated that his pseudonymous assailant was a High Church Tory pamphleteer (John Partridge to Isaac Manley, 24 April 1708; *CW* i. 189–90). So Swift sought to put an end to these impertinent signs of life in the deceased, publishing a new work entitled *A Vindication of Isaac Bickerstaff Esq; Against What is Objected to Him by Mr Partridge, in his Almanack for the Present Year 1709. By the said Isaac Bickerstaff Esq* (1709).

Whether or not Partridge lives is 'a Point meerly speculative'. Partridge's objection that he is alive demonstrates, says Bickerstaff, 'how much Men are blinded by their own Partiality ... he is the *only* Person from whom I ever heard that Objection offered'. Obvious bias discredits Partridge's claim. The *Vindication* contends, on stylistic grounds, 'that Mr *Partrige* is not alive'. Readers of Partridge's almanac exclaim that they *'were sure no Man* alive *ever writ such damned Stuff as this'*. It is conceded, however, that there may be 'an *uninformed* Carcass' still walking about calling itself Partridge. If Partridge has revived, that does not contradict the fact that he died as foretold by Bickerstaff (*PW* ii. 159–63). The grave or deadpan exposition of the outrageous or absurd in this pamphlet is characteristic of Swiftian ironic humour. In *The Accomplishment of the First of Mr Bickerstaff's Predictions*, Bickerstaff is said to have been mistaken by almost four hours in the time of Partridge's death (*PW* ii. 155). This is contested in the *Vindication*; Bickerstaff has been assured that he in fact computed the time of death 'to something under half an Hour' (*PW* ii. 163). Readers experience the ironic vertigo of a fictional writer correcting another fictional writer on a point of detail about a fictional death. Swift commemorated Partridge's 'death' with an elegy and epitaph (*Poems*, 93–6). Years later, when Dean of St Patrick's, Swift's main course on the cathedral feast day included partridges.[3]

Partridge, as an almanac-maker, did die for a few years. In 1709 Partridge sought to publish his almanac for 1710 independently of the Company of Stationers, which claimed the exclusive right to such publications. The verdict in the court case that ensued found in favour of the monopolistic privileges of the Company and Partridge was prohibited from printing his almanac. For the contemporary press this was further proof that Partridge was dead, as reported in Swift's Bickerstaff pamphlets. Partridge published a pamphlet explaining that he was alive and that the injunction against him printing his almanac had nothing to do with false reports of his death. It was five years before Partridge returned to print in an almanac. The *'Dead Man'*, as he called himself, condemned Swift as the notorious author of the Bickerstaff pamphlets.[4]

Swift derides Partridge as a 'cobbler, star-monger, and quack' (*Poems*, 96), but there was an ideological motivation for Swift's meticulously premeditated satiric kill. Partridge was an anticlerical Whig and, before Swift delivered his finishing stroke, had been the target of Tory satirists like Tom Brown and Ned Ward and had been satirized in the Tory version of Boccalini's *Advertisements from Parnassus*.[5] Partridge's almanac *Merlinus Liberatus* was dated from the Revolution of 1688 ('our Deliverance by K. William from Popery and Arbitrary Government') and from the failed Jacobite Assassination Plot of 1696 ('the Horrid Popish Jacobite Plot'). Partridge's *Merlinus Liberatus: Being an Almanack for . . . 1708* is introduced with a poem praising 'The Glorious *Union*' of England and Scotland in 1707. Swift wrote a poem and a pamphlet in 1707 denouncing the Union ('Verses Said to be Written on the Union', *Poems*, 92–3, and 'The Story of the Injured Lady', *PW* ix. 3–12). Partridge in his 'Observations' for July 1708 pronounced that Ireland was 'in a good Condition' despite Jacobite reports to the contrary and clearly approves projected Whig changes there. In December 1708 Swift published a pamphlet against Whig attempts to repeal the Sacramental Test in Ireland (*PW* ii. 109–25). For Partridge, as for Daniel Defoe, whose *Shortest Way with the Dissenters* (1702) parodied the rhetoric of High Churchmen such as Henry Sacheverell, contemporary High Churchmen were persecutors:

> *High-Church!* The common Curse, the Nation's Shame.
> 'Tis only *Pop'ry* by another Name,
> The Shortest Way, Blood, Ruin to Excess,
> Sa——ll's Brimstone Church is nothing less.

> (quoted by Davis in *PW* ii, p. x)

Swift's satire on Partridge was prompted not just by the folly of astrology, as Swift saw it, but principally by the politics of the astrologer. On his deathbed in Swift's *Accomplishment*, Partridge 'declared himself a Nonconformist, and had a fanatick Preacher to be his spiritual Guide' (*PW* ii. 155). Swift's hoax killing of the astrologer was also a shortest way with a Dissenter.

AN ARGUMENT AGAINST ABOLISHING
CHRISTIANITY

In 1708 the high-profile Jacobite High Churchman Charles Leslie published *The Socinian Controversy Discuss'd*. In an 'Author's PREFACE' Leslie wrote that it was now *'necessary to appear in defence of the christian Faith, that it be not lost among us; and to give some check to these Socinian Pamphlets which swarm, through this City especially'.[6]* Socinianism (named after the Italian anti-Trinitarian Faustus Socinus) asserts the unity of the Godhead and denies the divinity of Christ, and is character-ized by its biblicism and its assertion of the rights of reason in matters of religion. It was a principal heresy troubling ortho-dox clergymen in the decades after the Revolution of 1688–9. It was excepted from toleration in the religious settlement of 1689, and was being attacked in High Church pamphlet literature in 1708, when Swift wrote *An Argument against Abolishing Christianity*, and in 1711, when the *Argument* was first printed in his *Miscellanies in Prose and Verse*. Prominent figures in the Whig intellectual elite were suspected of this heresy, including John Locke and Isaac Newton.[7] In 1695 Leslie had imputed Socinianism to the Williamite regime's Arch-bishop of Canterbury, John Tillotson: 'He is own'd by the *Atheistical* Wits of all *England*, as their true *Primate* and *Apostle*.' Tillotson's name is placed 'in the *Front* of their *Anti-Christian Harangues* in Print'.[8] Leslie's *The Socinian Controversy Discuss'd* in six parts voluminously answered principal Socinian works. Leslie represents the anti-Trinitarians as anti-Christian.[9] Swift's ironic satire *An Argument against Abolishing Christianity* is primarily a brilliant High Church intervention in the Socinian controversy, which is specifically invoked in the tract.

Swift's *Argument* for nominal Christianity in an anti-Chris-tian world borrows 'a Distinction from the Writers on the other Side, when they make a Difference between nominal and real *Trinitarians*' (*PW* ii. 27). The anti-Christian 'Writers on the other Side' are the Socinians or anti-Trinitarians. Swift is referring to such Socinian works as *A Discourse concerning the Nominal and Real Trinitarians* (1695) and *The Judgment of a Disinterested Person concerning the . . . Trinity* (1696), which had represented theological controversy about the Trinity within the Anglican Church as a controversy between tritheistic heretics (the 'realists') and disguised Socinians (the 'nominalists'). John Toland's notorious *Christianity not Mysterious* (1696), appropriating a distinction from John Locke, distinguished 'the *Nominal* from the *Real* Essence of a thing'.[10] Toland's book was said to have revived '*Socinian*' principles with an 'Antichristian' design.[11] For contemporary Socinian polemicists the Trinity was but a nominal term that they expressed willingness to keep while denying its reality. The putative author of Swift's *Argument*, the 'I' of the tract, is a nominal Christian and a modern Whig. He is a parody of the Socinian 'nominalist', an anti-Trinitarian who uses the anachronistic language of the Church on the Trinity. The nominal Trinitarian becomes a nominal Christian in Swift's pamphlet.

The content of this satire against an imaginary proposal to abolish Christianity consists of parodies of actual anti-Trinitarian and anticlerical arguments of the time. So, for example, an objection against nominal Christianity (reductively styled 'the Gospel System') and in favour of its abolition is 'that it obliges Men to the Belief of Things too difficult for Free-Thinkers, and such who have shaken off the Prejudices that usually cling to a confined Education' (*PW* ii. 29). Leslie in the sixth Dialogue of *The Socinian Controversy Discuss'd* presents the Socinian spokesman as arguing 'That the Doctrin of the *Trinitarians* is no *Necessary* or *Fundamental* Doctrine of Christianity'. A reason offered is 'That it is *Difficult* to be *Understood*'. Leslie's Christian answers this objection: 'So is the Nature of God. The most Learned have very obscure and imperfect Notions of it, and some common People have even Blasphemous and Contradictory Apprehensions of *God*. Yet you wou'd not exclude the *Belief of a God* from being a *Fundamental Article*.'[12] In Swift's *Argument* it is the very belief in God that is being rejected as 'too difficult' to be understood. Swift is parodying as atheism anti-Trinitarian objections against the Trinitarian conception of God that it was logically incomprehensible. One Socinian author after examining the orthodox exegesis of the Trinity concluded that it was '*Egyptian* all over'.[13] The Socinian writer Stephen Nye argued that a doctrine as uncertain and obscure as the Trinity was not a fundamental doctrine of Christianity but 'Prejudices of Education ... and Fear of Penalties' have made men assent to it. The anticlerical Matthew Tindal in a Socinian pamphlet ridiculed the clergy's illogical adoration of 'the number Three'.[14] The Socinian pamphlet *A Discourse concerning the Nominal and Real Trinitarians* typically contended that, if all the Trinitarian terms 'were abolished', it 'would heal all our breaches, and perfectly restore our peace, not only in this, but in (almost) all other questions and strifes'.[15] The great advantage claimed for the abolition of nominal Christianity in Swift's satire is 'that it will utterly extinguish Parties among us, by removing those factious Distinctions of High and Low Church, of *Whig* and *Tory, Presbyterian* and *Church-of-England'*, an unlikely prospect argues the nominalist speaker (*PW* ii. 31, 32). The *Argument*'s apology for and defence of a nominal Christianity parodies Socinian cynicism. Just as the contemporary anti-Trinitarian will allow the retention of the Church's Trinitarian language precisely because the signification is verbal only, the nominalist speaker of the *Argument* advises the retention of nominal Christianity on the grounds that religion has been extirpated and the Christian terms are merely harmless words (*PW* ii. 33–4).

The satire presents the High Church nightmare of a materialist and nominalist world where Christianity is merely a set of terms, its creed and doctrines having no essential meaning. If lip service is paid to Christianity, it is for irreligious reasons. Swift's satiric parody of Socinianism and excoriating exposure of an irreligious world is also an ironic defence of the nominal terms of the Established faith. Swift's nominalist finds politic reasons for preserving Christianity in name only. The sardonic assumption of the tract is that in Socinian and atheistic 1708 it would be futile to attempt a defence of real Christianity. In the *Miscellanies* of 1711 this ironic tract was placed between two works of religious orthodoxy, *The Sentiments of a Church-of-England Man* and *A Project for the Advancement of Religion*, as if to frame the irony and parody of the *Argument*. There are echoes and parallels between the three works. One of Swift's few surviving sermons, 'On the Trinity', provides an extended defence of the Anglican Church's catholic orthodoxy on the doctrine of the Trinity (*PW* ix. 159–68). Swift suspected that Socinian proceedings against 'the famous doctrine of Christ's divinity' were a design to 'abolish that religion altogether' (*PW* ix. 261). But for Swift the best form of defence in print was satiric attack.

The fictive world of the *Argument*, where Christianity has been removed, reflects Swift's deep pessimism about the contemporary state of the kingdom. In a letter to Archbishop King in January 1709, Swift wrote:

> I compare true Religion to Learning and Civility which have ever been in the World, but very often shifted their Scenes, sometimes entirely leaving whole Countries where they have long flourished, and removing to others that before were barbarous, which hath been the Case of Christianity itself, particularly in many parts of Africa, and how far the Wickedness of a Nation may provoke God Almighty to inflict so great a Judgment, is terrible to think. (*CW* i. 226)

The fears about the future of Christianity, and the nightmare fantasy of an irreligious world where Christianity is only nominal imagined in the *Argument* of 1708, seemed to have materialized in Hanoverian Britain. When the clergy's right to collect tithes was threatened by the Irish and English parliaments in the 1730s, Swift predicted that it was the end of Christianity. In 1736 Swift told a Catholic Jacobite abroad 'that those wretches here, who call themselves a parliament, abhor the clergy of our church, more than those of yours, and have made an universal association to defraud us of our undoubted dues' (*Corr.* iv. 469). He declared to his friend Charles Ford that 'I am heartily sick of the worst times and Peoples, and Oppressions that History can shew in either Kingdom'. The survival of the Church and Christianity was in question: 'I have long given up all hopes of Church and Christianity. A certain Author (I forget his name,) hath writ a book (I wish I could see it) that the Christian Religion will not last above 300 and odd years. He means, there will always be Christians, as there are Jews; but it will be no longer a Nationall Religion.' The Church 'is equally the Aversion of both Kingdoms' (*Corr.* iv. 504–5). Other High Churchmen shared Swift's pessimism. *An Argument against Abolishing Christianity* offered a model of satiric irony for High Church pamphlet literature on Erastian Whig parliaments and heterodox anticlericalism. The nonjuror

John Hildrop's ironic pamphlet *A Letter to a Member of Parliament, Containing a Proposal for Bringing in a Bill to Revise, Amend or Repeal Certain Obsolete Statutes, Commonly called The Ten Commandments*, published anonymously by a High Church printer, presents the Ten Commandments as anachronistic and textually corrupt. These obsolete laws must be abolished by an enlightened legislature: 'as the happy Inhabitants of these reformed Nations have long ago got rid of all the superstitious Impositions of Christian Priestcraft, it is a Shame and Reproach to them to be still in Bondage to *Jewish* Ordinances.'[16]

A MODEST PROPOSAL

Imagining Whig enormities in ecclesiastical affairs as a project to abolish Christianity, Swift portrayed their regime in Ireland as genocidal. *A Modest Proposal for Preventing the Children of Poor People from being a Burthen to their Parents, or the Country, and for Making them Beneficial to the Publick* (1729), Swift's cold-blooded and clinically executed ironic satire on the Irish poor and their oppressors, identifies the Hanoverian Whig establishment in Ireland with a proposal to exterminate the poor. The work was understood by Swift's English Jacobite Tory friends, Lord Bathurst and the Second Earl of Oxford, as a disaffected attack on the English Whig administration, which had devoured Ireland and would soon consume an impoverished England (*Corr.* iii. 372–3, 403–4; v. 78–9). The trope of a devouring Whig government was familiar in the Opposition political press of the period.[17] A Jacobite ideologist had even put the case of a sovereign who forces his subjects 'to eat one another' as one in which the removal of a king would be justifiable.[18]

The putative author, the 'Modest Proposer', reveals himself to be a Protestant Whig member of the established settler class. He is fanatically anti-Jacobite, indeed paranoid about the Stuart Pretender, and is sympathetic to Protestant Dissenters from the Established Church of Ireland. The Modest Proposer complains that the Catholic Irish 'leave their *dear Native Country, to fight for the Pretender in* Spain'. Yet he also complains that the Irish stay in Ireland 'on Purpose, with a

Design to *deliver the Kingdom to the Pretender*; hoping to take their Advantage by the Absence *of so many good Protestants*, who have chosen rather to leave their Country, than stay at home, and pay Tithes against their Conscience, to an idolatrous *Episcopal Curate'* (*PW* xii. 109, 114). The putative author's modest proposal, as is eventually revealed in the ninth paragraph, after some opening paragraphs on the problem of Irish poverty, is that the solution to Irish poverty is to process the children of the poor into a financial, nutritional, and culinary asset by eating them. It is silently assumed that nobody in Ireland or England would think eating people is wrong or that such a proposal was monstrously inhumane. Swift twists the ironic knife further, for this cannibal final solution is not to be regarded as more horrific than what the Irish poor currently endure, indeed it might be seen as preferable:

> I desire those Politicians, who dislike my Overture, and may perhaps be so bold to attempt an Answer, that they will first ask the Parents of these Mortals, Whether they would not, at this Day, think it a great Happiness to have been sold for Food at a Year old, in the Manner I prescribe; and thereby have avoided such a perpetual Scene of Misfortunes, as they have since gone through; by the *Oppression of Landlords*; the Impossibility of paying Rent, without Money or Trade; the Want of common Sustenance, with neither House nor Cloaths, to cover them from the Inclemencies of Weather; and the most inevitable Prospect of intailing the like, or greater Miseries upon their Breed for ever. (*PW* xii. 117–18)

Swift regarded contemporary Ireland as in a uniquely horrific situation of poverty and famine, where human life had no value. The Modest Proposer says 'that I calculate my Remedy *for this one individual Kingdom of* IRELAND, *and for no other that ever was, is, or I think ever can be upon Earth*' (*PW* xii. 116). *A Modest Proposal* is deliberately sensational. Only an unthinkable proposal and the black humour of satiric fantasy could suggest the unspeakable and unimaginable horror of Hanoverian Ireland.

The title of the pamphlet imitates the titles of serious contemporary proposals in political economy.[19] But the word 'Modest' in the title might well have contained an ironic hint for contemporaries that they should be prepared for some immoral monstrosity of Whig provenance. The anticlerical Whig Bernard Mandeville had scandalized conventional morality with a proposal for the toleration of prostitution and establishment of state-controlled brothels entitled *A Modest Defence of Publick Stews* (1724). Indeed, Mandeville's speaker ('a Layman') anticipates the manner of Swift's Modest Proposer in his moral amnesia, unemotional utilitarianism, and cool calculation of the side-benefits of the scheme. Like the Modest Proposer, Mandeville's speaker is attentive to detail: 'No Woman that has been twice pox'd shall ever be re-admitted' to a public brothel 'Note, That three Claps shall be reckon'd equivalent to one Pox'.[20] Swift had already parodied another of Mandeville's memorable titles (*The Fable of the Bees: or, Private Vices, Publick Benefits* (1714)) when he told Archbishop King in 1721 that a proposal for an Irish bank 'was for private advantage and public mischief'.[21] Swift exhorted the Irish to prefer 'the public interest to their present private advantage' (*PW* ix. 237).[22] Swift was a searing satirist of the phenomenon known in the late-twentieth and early twenty-first centuries as 'privatization' and relentlessly exposed cases where he felt the public interest had been sacrificed for private advantage.[23] The final irony in *A Modest Proposal* is in the ethical proof offered by the Modest Proposer for the public-spirited motives behind his genocidal scheme to eat Irish babies. At the end of the pamphlet, the Modest Proposer claims to be without private views: 'I have no Children, by which I can propose to get a single Penny; the youngest being nine years old, and my Wife past Child-bearing' (*PW* xii. 118). However, the Modest Proposer does have an eye on his own posterity. There is a hint, at the beginning of the pamphlet, that he feels he deserves to have 'his Statue set up for a Preserver of the Nation' (*PW* xii. 109). The Modest Proposer also rejects a proposed refinement on his cannibal project, put forward by a fellow patriot, which was to use 'the Bodies of young Lads and Maidens, not exceeding fourteen Years of Age, nor under twelve' as substitutes for venison, since gentlemen have over-hunted and destroyed all their deer. The ostensible reasons given for the rejection of this refinement are the lean toughness of the flesh of the males, and the '*Loss to the Publick*' of a capital asset in destroying females just as they are about to become 'Breeders'. The objection of 'Cruelty' is also entertained for the first and last time (*PW* xii. 113). However, the Modest Proposer's later disclosure that he has a 9-year-old child hints at his private motive for rejecting the shooting of early adolescents: he is not prepared to put in place a scheme in which he would be sacrificing his own child in the near future. The Modest Proposer exemplifies Whig hegemony: private self-interest and public evil.

Swift said that the 'whiggish or fanatical Genius' among the English interest in Ireland derived from the time of Cromwell (*PW* ix. 30–1) and this satire grimly invokes cultural memories of Cromwellian massacre, as well as accounts of cannibalism among the Irish poor during times of famine.[24] The Modest Proposer is a fanatical Whig genius planning to massacre the starving Irish poor. Swift's satire is also exploiting an old imputation that is succinctly described by Charles Wogan, an Irish Catholic Jacobite exile, in a letter to Swift of 27 February 1733. Wogan wrote: 'Our English ancestors dispatched into Ireland, and their descendants, have taken effectual care to fasten this bugbear upon their mother country, and represent the Irish as monstors and cannibals, in order to justify their own more barbarous oppressions upon that people'.[25] Swift's satiric pamphlet imputes cannibalism to the oppressors as well as to the Irish poor. Swift's satire also activates an old claim, found, like the cannibal imputation, in Edmund Spenser's anti-Irish, English colonialist treatise *A View of the State of Ireland* (completed by 1598, first published 1633), that the Irish are descended from the Scythians, an ancient, barbaric, and nomadic tribe who inhabited a region north of the Black Sea. The by-products of the Modest Proposer's cannibal scheme (a child's skin 'artificially dressed, will make admirable *Gloves for Ladies*, and *Summer Boots for fine Gentlemen*' (*PW* xii. 112)) recall accounts in Herodotus and Strabo of the Scythians producing luxury goods from human skin and bone. Swift also alludes to his own work, recalling Lemuel Gulliver's account in part IV of *Gulliver's Travels* of using the skins of humanoid Yahoos for sails and clothing and Yahoo tallow for his boat.[26] In Swift's satire the Irish settler elite and the Hanoverian establishment for which the Modest Proposer speaks are as cannibal and savagely Scythian as the Irish poor they oppress.

As with the cannibal and Scythian imputations, so the English characterization of the Irishman as 'a valuable slave in our western plantations, where they are distinguished by the ignominious epithet of White Negroes'[27] is replicated in *A Modest Proposal* but given wider satiric application and precise political charge. The Modest Proposer says that the only current prospects for the Irish poor are to 'turn *Thieves* for want of Work', to join the Jacobite regiments abroad, or to 'sell themselves to the *Barbadoes*' (*PW* xii. 109). The Modest Proposer had thought of turning the children of the Irish poor into slaves rather than food:

> I AM assured by our Merchants, that a Boy or a Girl before twelve Years old, is no saleable Commodity; and even when they come to this Age, they will not yield above Three Pounds, or Three Pounds and half a Crown at most, on the Exchange; which cannot turn to Account either to the Parents or the Kingdom; the Charge of Nutriment and Rags, having been at least four Times that Value. (*PW* xii. 111)

The Modest Proposer here shares what Swift regarded as the views of Ireland's enslavers, the landlord class and the English Whig government. In his sermon on the 'Causes of the Wretched Condition of Ireland', Swift refers to 'that *Ægyptian* Bondage of cruel, oppressing, covetous Landlords, expecting that all who live under them should *make Bricks without Straw* . . . by which the Spirits of the People are broken, and made for Slavery' (*PW* ix. 201). In *A Short View of the State of Ireland*, first printed in 1728, the year before the publication of *A Modest Proposal*, and reprinted in part in the crypto-Jacobite Tory *Mist's Weekly Journal* in London, it is England and the Hanoverian king who are the slave masters. Ireland is denied liberties enjoyed by 'the meanest Prince in the *German* Empire' and, alluding to Exodus 5: 17, the Irish are imaged as the Israelites suffering under their Pharoah: '*YE are idle, ye are idle*, answered *Pharoah* to the *Israelites*, when they complained to *his Majesty*, that they were forced to make Bricks without Straw' (*PW* xii. 11–12). Swift had written that it was under the administration of the extreme Whig Lord Lieutenant of Ireland, Thomas, Earl of Wharton, in 1708–10, that steps were taken 'towards finishing the Slavery of that People' (*PW* iii.

177–8). In Swift's virulent *Short Character* of Wharton, 'collaterally' is a Wharton word (*PW* iii. 184). The Whig Modest Proposer speaks of the 'Collateral Advantage' of his cannibal scheme in 'lessening the Number of *Papists* among us' (*PW* xii. 112).

Swift claimed that his counter-hegemonic writing and activism were 'owing to perfect rage and resentment, and the mortifying sight of slavery, folly, and baseness about me' (*Corr.* iii. 289). He wrote that 'What I did for this Country was from perfect Hatred of Tyranny and Oppression' (*PW* xiii. 112). Swift's polemic and satire in defence of Ireland did not just condemn the enslavers; he represents Ireland's native population as vicious, brutalized slaves. He typically writes of 'the poor Popish Natives' with contempt and complains that they only contribute to their slavery (*PW* ix. 209). Some of Swift's real remedies for the Irish problem are conveniently listed in italics near the end of *A Modest Proposal* as 'other Expedients' that seem to have no hope of implementation (*PW* xii. 116–17). Dismissed as impractical by the Modest Proposer, these expedients all focus on what the Irish could be doing domestically to alleviate their plight but are not. While Swift expresses antipathy for the vicious and improvident Irish poor, he did express esteem for the Irish Jacobite diaspora, praising Jacobite soldiers in Spanish service abroad, the very men who represented the only military option for overturning this English Hanoverian Whig tyranny and oppression in Ireland (*Corr.* iv. 51). The Whig Modest Proposer by contrast is scandalized that some of the Irish 'leave their *dear Native Country, to fight for the Pretender in* Spain' (*PW* xii. 109).

Swift produced a large corpus of writings on Ireland opposing English oppression and proposing various self-help schemes for the Irish. It was the failure of these 'other Expedients' that led him in exasperation to propose, ironically, a singular remedy so shocking that it would arrest the attention of the political nation to the plight of Ireland. In his other writings on Ireland, such as his sermon on the 'Causes of the Wretched Condition of Ireland', Swift wrote that rack-renting, absentee landlords 'draw out the very Vitals of their Mother Kingdom'. These 'cruel Landlords are every Day unpeopling their Kingdom' (*PW* ix. 200, 201). In *A Short View of the State of Ireland* (1728) he writes that the 'Rise of our Rents is squeezed out of the very Blood, and Vitals, and Cloaths, and Dwellings of the Tenants; who live worse than *English* Beggars' (*PW* xii. 11). Swift as Drapier excoriates the *'Blood-suckers'* (*PW* x. 7). What were merely tropes in Swift's other Irish pamphlets are literalized in *A Modest Proposal*. In non-ironic proposals on Irish political economy, Swift called for Irish consumption of 'the growth and manufacture of this kingdom' (*PW* xii. 127). This familiar exhortation, in *A Modest Proposal*, is literally closer to the bone, pitched with black humour. The Modest Proposer observes that in his scheme for a cannibal economy 'the Goods' are 'entirely of our own Growth and Manufacture' (*PW* xii. 115). Swift's sardonic technique, of taking *'Hyperboles* in too literal a Sense' (*PW* ii. 13), was one that had sensational effect when Defoe used it in *The Shortest Way with the Dissenters*, a scandalous ironic pamphlet of 1702, which parodied the extremism of High Church Tory rhetoric against the Dissenters as literal calls to massacre them. Swift's sensational pamphlet imagines the Whig masters and slaves in Ireland collaborating in cannibal murder. The High Churchman, however, did think of the shortest way with the Irish in a more literal sense in other pamphlets. Swift writes in *A Short View of the State of Ireland* that 'I have often wished, that a Law were enacted to hang up half a Dozen *Bankers* every Year; and thereby interpose at least some short Delay, to the further Ruin of *Ireland*' (*PW* xii. 11). Vagabond beggars in Dublin are 'fitter to be rooted out of the Face of the Earth, than suffered to levy a vast annual Tax upon the City' (*A Proposal for Giving Badges to the Beggars*, *PW* xiii. 139).

Swift said that in writing general satire the satirist should have particular instances in view. The satire of *A Modest Proposal* had particular Whig personalities in its sights. The Allens, a Dublin mercantile family who were staunchly Williamite and Hanoverian Whig in politics, are a particular target in *A Modest Proposal*, as elsewhere in Swift's writing. In his poem 'Traulus', an attack on Joshua, second Viscount Allen, Swift satirized the Whig family as butchers and wrote that the Viscount 'draws his daily food, | From his tenants' vital blood' (ll. 41–2; *Poems*, 426). The punishment of 'Traulus' meted out by the satirist in a pamphlet of 1730 is to imagine him flayed and dissected alive and the carcase put on display for threepence (*PW* xii. 157–8). Allen's grandfather was a Lord Mayor of Dublin and an exporter of salt meat. In places the Modest Proposer seems to be addressing the Whig grandee when he outlines the benefits of his cannibal scheme: 'a well-grown fat yearling Child . . . roasted whole, will make a considerable Figure at a *Lord Mayor's Feast,* or any other publick Entertainment' (*PW* xii. 116). In a passage where Swift palpably erupts from behind the ironic pose of the Modest Proposer, pro-English salt meat exporters are reassured about the human meat trade: 'we can incur no Danger in *disobliging* ENGLAND: For, this Kind of Commodity will not bear Exportation; the Flesh being of too tender a Consistence, to admit a long Continuance in Salt; *although, perhaps, I could name a Country, which would be glad to eat up our whole Nation without it'* (*PW* xii. 117).

It is assumed by the Modest Proposer that the only objection readers will have to his cannibal proposal is a culinary one, and the Modest Proposer, significantly, is *au fait* with French dishes: 'a young healthy Child, well nursed, is, at a Year old, a most delicious, nourishing, and wholesome Food; whether *Stewed, Roasted, Baked,* or *Boiled*; and, I make no doubt, that it will equally serve in a *Fricasie,* or *Ragoust* (*PW* xii. 111). This black humour is more than just a satire on the luxury of the rich. Its topical target is the gourmandizing grandees of the Hanoverian Whig government who were devouring Ireland. The Whig first or Prime Minister Robert Walpole employed French cooks. A sign of English Whig power was its culinary style, and among the elite dishes upon which the Whig ministers notoriously fed were the olio, fricassee, and ragout. Attacks on Whig French luxury (and emphasis on the Stuart Pretender's love of plain English fare, even though he was exiled in Italy) were staples of Jacobite opposition propaganda.[28] Swift may have already been alerted to this political trope by the work of the Jacobite Matthias Earbery, who had criticized Lemuel Gulliver for not giving a full report on the kitchens of the courts in the countries he visits.[29] In *A Modest Proposal* the sign of Whig hegemony is its obscene cuisine.

It is insinuated that the Whig court and ministry might even refine their taste further in line with oriental cruelty. Citing as his authority 'the famous *Salmanaazor*, a Native of the Island *Formosa*' (in fact a notorious French imposter who claimed to be a Formosan), the Modest Proposer reports that 'the Body of a plump Girl of fifteen' was a 'prime Dainty' sold to the Formosan 'Imperial *Majesty's prime Minister of State*, and other great *Mandarins* of the Court, *in Joints from the Gibbet*, at Four hundred Crowns' (*PW* xii. 113–14). Swift's satire, however, pans from the cannibal imperial court and ministry to focus its animus on the court's victims: 'Neither indeed can I deny, that if the same Use were made of several plump young girls in this Town, who, without one single Groat to their Fortunes, cannot stir Abroad without a Chair, and appear at the *Play-house*, and *Assemblies* in foreign Fineries, which they never will pay for; the Kingdom would not be the worse' (*PW* xii. 114). This is Swiftian cauterizing of what he saw as a principal corruption in Ireland: consumption of foreign commodities, particularly the fetishistic preference for foreign-made clothes. The satiric animus against Irish luxury in Swift's other writings, as in *A Modest Proposal*, is refracted through a misogynist and misanthropic lens. In *A Modest Proposal* it is the bodies of plump young girls in foreign fineries who should be disjointed and eaten. Other writings direct considerable violence against women who spend the entire family revenue 'to adorn a nauseous unwholesom living Carcase' (*PW* xii. 80) and against men who 'cannot find Materials in their own Country worthy to adorn their Bodies of Clay' (*PW* ix. 201).

The linguistic violence of *A Modest Proposal* – the dehumanizing diction in which the Irish are referred to as beasts for instance – vents Swift's own animus against the improvident and vicious poor and against the land of his birth, as critics such as Claude Rawson have shown. The Modest Proposer speaks of 'a Child, *just dropt from its Dam*' and tells us that Irish adults would think it a great happiness to have been slaughtered as yearlings rather than suffer as they have in Ireland (*PW* xii. 110, 117). Swift would express similar sentiments about the land of his birth in a letter to the Earl of Oxford in 1737: 'I happened to be dropped here, and was a Year old before I left it, and to my Sorrow did not dye before I came back to it again' (*Corr.* v. 46–7). The Modest Proposer's representation of the Irish as beasts is not so different from

Swift's own non-ironic statements in works such as his sermon on the 'Causes of the Wretched Condition of Ireland' (*PW* ix. 199–209) and his later *A Proposal for Giving Badges to the Beggars* (1737; *PW* xiii. 131–40), where Swift's punitive severity towards vagabond beggars and violent diminution in diction are on stark display. The Modest Proposer's sentimental expressions of compassion for the poor, especially in the opening paragraph of the pamphlet, are bogus of course. He plans to kill them. The point is that professions of sympathy coming from Ireland's rulers are an obscene hypocrisy. The 'poor Popish Natives' deserve rebuke more than pity. Swift certainly had a harder view of the poor. The Modest Proposer refers to beggars *'all in Rags'* (*PW* xii. 109). Swift wrote in his *Proposal for Giving Badges to the Beggars* that 'their Rags are Part of their Tools' (*PW* xiii. 140). The Modest Proposer nonchalantly comments:

> SOME Persons of a desponding Spirit are in great Concern about that vast Number of poor People, who are Aged, Diseased, or Maimed ... But I am not in the least Pain upon that Matter; because it is very well known, that they are every Day *dying*, and *rotting*, by *Cold* and *Famine*, and *Filth*, and *Vermin*, as fast as can be reasonably expected. (*PW* xii. 114)

Offering a 'very plain Proposal' under his own name, Swift in the *Proposal for Giving Badges to the Beggars* calls for vagabond beggars to be whipped back to the parishes from which they came and charity refused them: 'As for the Aged and Infirm, it would be sufficient to give them nothing, and then they must starve or follow their Brethren' (*PW* xiii. 132, 138). In *A Modest Proposal*, the Irish are innately vicious, and readers are not offered a different frame of reference. The ethnography in the pamphlet merely confirms the Modest Proposer's account of the Irish problem. In a brilliant exhibition of satiric syntax in the following passage, qualifying clauses unexpectedly accentuate the slur that the Irish are thieves. The passage quietly assumes that all Irish natives over 6 years of age are thieves and the qualifying clauses indicate that anyone under 6 is either a thief or an apprentice thief:

> They can very seldom pick up a Livelyhood *by Stealing* until they arrive at six Years old; except where they are of towardly Parts;

although, I confess, they learn the Rudiments much earlier; during which Time, they can, however, be properly looked upon as *Probationers*; as I have been informed by a principal Gentleman in the County of *Cavan*, who protested to me, that he never knew above one or two Instances under the Age of six, even in a Part of the Kingdom *so renowned for the quickest Proficiency in that Art.* (*PW* xii. 111)

A Modest Proposal might even be seen as one of the authorities for *A Proposal for Giving Badges to the Beggars* when Swift declares that the vagabond Irish beggar 'and his Female are Thieves, and teach the Trade of stealing to their Brood at four Years old' (*PW* xiii. 134). In exposing the devouring ruling class for whom the Modest Proposer speaks, the Dean of St Patrick's is not saying that the mendicant poor are innocent victims who deserve our sympathy.

A Modest Proposal is Swift's jeremiad against the Irish and their oppressors. Swift's use of the cannibal theme has biblical resonance, alluding particularly to God's foreshadowing of his judgement on the Jews and the destruction of Jerusalem in Jeremiah 19: 9: 'I will cause them to eat the flesh of their sons and the flesh of their daughters, and they shall eat every one the flesh of his friend in the siege and straitness, wherewith their enemies, and they that seek their lives, shall straiten them.' *A Modest Proposal* identifies the self-destructive Irish with the Jews oppressed by the Romans, and Swift exhorts them not to '*act any longer like the* Jews, *who were murdering one another at the very Moment their City was taken*' (*PW* xii. 116). Swift alludes to passages in Josephus' well-known account of the siege and destruction of Jerusalem by Titus in AD 70, which describes the Jews as fighting among themselves and murdering each other before and during the Roman attack. Josephus' description of the horror of the famine among the Jews in the city in AD 70 includes accounts of cannibalism.[30] The siege of Jerusalem and the account of cannibalism had an exemplary significance as a prototype of later European horrors, of which Ireland under Hanoverian Whig government is for Swift the home-grown case.[31] Swift wrote another tract in the character of the loyal Whig Modest Proposer. In *The Answer to the Craftsman* (*PW* xii. 173–8) the Modest Proposer looks forward to Ireland becoming 'a new *Arcadia*' under British policies: the

53

depopulated colony in the British archipelago, entirely dependent on England, inhabited by a few vegetarians grazing export cattle for English butchers.

4

Gulliver's Travels

Travels into Several Remote Nations of the World. In Four Parts by Lemuel Gulliver, First a Surgeon and then a Captain of several Ships, first published in 1726 and then in a revised edition in 1735, is seditious in its political implication and misanthropic in its satiric project. In a famous letter to Alexander Pope of 29 September 1725, Swift wrote that his 'Travells' were 'intended for the press when the world shall deserve them, or rather when a Printer shall be found brave enough to venture his Eares' (loss of ears was a traditional punishment for sedition). The 'Travells', he told Pope, were built upon a 'great foundation of Misanthropy (though not Timons manner)' (*CW* ii. 606–7). *Gulliver's Travels* (as the work has come to be known) is extraordinarily entertaining. The reader is taken in unpredictable directions in these voyages and the comedy ranges from innocent amusement to violent adults-only black humour. It is also a work of genuine extremism. The seditious edge and misanthropic animus will be described in this chapter, which will also re-examine the relationship between Swift and Gulliver, and the nagging problem of the Houyhnhnms.

Gulliver's Travels belongs to a European literary tradition of satiric and utopian imaginary voyages. Important landmarks in this literary tradition include Lucian's *True History*, Thomas More's *Utopia*, Rabelais's *Gargantua and Pantagruel*, and Joseph Hall's *Mundus Alter et Idem* (*Another World and Yet the Same*), a voyage to four imaginary places. Voyage literature was in great vogue in the early eighteenth century and Swift has hijacked the popular genre, parodying the travel book and converting it into a vehicle for satire. The voyage to a remote place afforded Swift a narrative scaffolding for his satire and an estranging or defamiliarizing device. Gulliver is separated from his own kind at the beginning of each voyage, either through shipwreck, abandonment, hijack, or mutiny and then observes or is told about alternative social and political models in the countries he visits. He witnesses the corruptions of his own country mirrored in the disreputable aspects of the remote peoples with whom he comes in contact. Gulliver visits remote places, but the satirist exposes home truths about human folly and depravity. Gulliver's own society is scrutinized from different perspectives. In part I it is mocked by being mimicked by the petty and contemptible Lilliputians. In part II it is diminished as Lilliputian in the view of giants. In part III it is derided in the various intellectual, social, and political abuses Gulliver witnesses as he goes island hopping. In part IV European society is anatomized as an anthropological Other in the Houyhnhnm master's ethnographic account of Yahoo behaviour and it is demystified and dissected in the conversations between Gulliver and his Houyhnhnm master. The fable of part IV deepens the satire on the 'degenerate Nature of Man' (I. vi. 60) displayed in the early books, and given hideous corporeal particularity in the immortal Struldbruggs of part III who embody 'that continual Degeneracy of human Nature' (III. x. 210). The moral of the fable in part IV is that humans are not rational animals but worse than unreasoning brutes.

The contemporary travel book as well as being a convenient frame for the satire also offered important targets. In the egoism of contemporary first-person voyage accounts Swift found modern hubris writ large, which this mock-travel book punctures through satiric pastiche and parody. *Gulliver's Travels* particularly parodies personal highlights and incidents in the texts of high-profile voyagers such as Lionel Wafer and William Dampier (Gulliver's 'Cousin', *PW* xi. 5).[1] For example, in his *A New Voyage and Description of the Isthmus of America* (1699), Wafer reported that he had saved a native woman's life, one of the King's wives, by blood-letting, though 'this rash attempt had like to have cost me my Life'. However, such was the reputation he gained by his success, Wafer says the King 'bowed, and kiss'd my Hand. Then the rest came thick about me, and some kissed my Hand, others my Knee, and some my Foot . . . the *Indians* . . . in a manner ador'd me.'² In stark contrast, Gulliver is abject and servile before the authority figures in the remote places he visits. It is Gulliver who does the prostration and foot kissing in Swift's book (see, for example, II. iii. 101; III. ix. 204–5). In part IV Swiftian humiliation of the voyager elides into an insult to human nature. About to depart from Houyhnhnmland, Gulliver takes leave of his Houyhnhnm master:

> But as I was going to prostrate myself to kiss his Hoof, he did me the Honour to raise it gently to my Mouth. I am not ignorant how much I have been censured for mentioning this last Particular. Detractors are pleased to think it improbable, that so illustrious a Person should descend to give so great a Mark of Distinction to a Creature so inferior as I. Neither have I forgot, how apt some Travellers are to boast of extraordinary Favours they have received. (IV. x. 282)

Swift not only has Gulliver kissing a horse's hoof and thinking himself unworthy of the honour, but the passage is so framed that it is assumed readers will not believe Gulliver's account because they know human nature is too inferior to be complimented in this way.

Gulliver also reports an incident, echoing Wafer, 'which had like to have cost me my Life'. In part II he slips through the fingers of a Brobdingnagian Governess and would have fallen to his death if 'I had not been stop'd by a Corking-pin that stuck in the good Gentlewoman's Stomacher'. He was suspended in mid-air with the head of the pin catching him 'between my Shirt and the Waistband of my Breeches' (II. v. 121). The proud voyager is impaled in the satire as a ludicrous figure. Wafer reported in his narrative that he injured his knee and he gives an extended account of his suffering. Although the injured knee is cured, Wafer informs the reader that there is 'a Weakness in that Knee, which remain'd long after, and a Benummedness which I sometimes find in it to this Day'.³ In an encounter with the natives of New Holland that is a pastiche of Wafer and of Dampier's account of a skirmish in New Holland, Gulliver is wounded, of course, in the knee, and Gulliver confides: '(I shall carry the Mark to my Grave)' (IV. xi.

57

284).[4] In Swift's parody of Dampier, quotidian torments become grotesque horrors. Dampier's accounts of the annoying flies in New Holland, for example, are magnified in Brobdingnag, where Gulliver is pestered by enormous flies, described in excremental detail (II. iii. 109).[5]

The diminution of travellers and parody of the genre were not Swift's only purposes in choosing the travel book as satiric vehicle. Voyage literature accounts of remote peoples were an important source for what High Church Tory writers regarded as a dangerous anthropological fantasy. This was the idea, found in the political theory of John Locke and the radical Whigs, that there existed a pre-social state of nature in which individuals were free and equal and that political authority was founded on the consent of free individuals in this independent state of nature.[6] In each remote country Gulliver visits there is government and subordination. All have monarchical government, except the non-human order of the Houyhnhnms. The institution of the patriarchal family appears to be universal. Gulliver's Houyhnhnm master thought 'Nature and Reason were sufficient Guides for a reasonable Animal' (IV. v. 248). The Houyhnhnms embody what the Jacobite ideologist Chevalier Ramsay described as 'the Idea' of a 'State ... conformable to reasonable Nature', the fictional 'Golden Age':

> IF Men, would follow the Law of Nature ... they would have no occasion for positive Laws, nor exemplary Punishments: Reason would be the common Law; Men would live in Simplicity without Pride, in mutual Commerce without Propriety, and in Equality without Jealousy: They would know no other Superiority but that of Virtue, nor no other Ambition but that of being generous and disinterested.

However, Ramsay, like Swift, thought 'Self-Love' and passions prevent humankind from living in such a state.[7] The Jacobite political philosopher thought government with a supreme power was necessary for humankind. Swift's state of nature is a non-human, hierarchical order, and even these equine Arcadians have a representative General Assembly with supreme power to which individual Houyhnhnms are subordinate. Challenging Whig political philosophy, Ramsay argued that '*All Men are born, more or less unequal*'. Some men 'by the Superiority of their Mind, Wisdom, Virtue and Valour, are born fit to govern, whilst there are a vast Number of others, who have not the like Talents' who are to obey. The 'Order of Nature' has contrived 'different natural Talents to support this Subordination'.[8] The Houyhnhnm master makes Gulliver observe 'that among the *Houyhnhnms*, the *White*, the *Sorrel*, and the *Iron-grey*, were not so exactly shaped as the *Bay*, the *Dapple-grey*, and the *Black*; nor born with equal Talents of Mind, or a Capacity to improve them; and therefore continued always in the Condition of Servants' (IV. vi. 256). As scholars have shown, the colour hierarchy of the Houyhnhnms in fact follows contemporary equine authorities in which the white and sorrel horses were ranked below the bay and the black. However, the hierarchical distinction among Swift's mythic horses also invites analogies with caste systems in authoritarian classical utopias such as Plato's *Republic* and the Ancient Sparta of the lawgiver Lycurgus. The inherent subordination in the Houyhnhnm state of nature is an intervention in contemporary political–philosophical debate, contradicting the idea of a natural state of equality and independency. The world Gulliver explores and the state of nature he witnesses are remote from Whig political philosophy.

Gulliver's Travels is a general satire on corruption in European societies, but it is also a topical political attack on the persons, principles, and proceedings of the Whig party regime that ruled Britain after 1714. The positives of the satire are reactionary and nostalgic in character. Old pre-degenerate Lilliput, which is modelled on 'the institutions of LUCURGUS' in Ancient Sparta, is clearly presented as admirable in part I (I. vi. 57–63).[9] The hereditary monarchy of Brobdingnag without faction and gunpowder is the 'least corrupted' of the human societies Gulliver visits: that monarchy's 'wise Maxims in Morality and Government, it would be our Happiness to observe' (IV. xii. 292). In part III, old-fashioned Lord Munodi, the '*Sextumvirate*' of worthies with only one modern in it (Sir Thomas More), and the '*English* Yeomen of the old Stamp' are valorized (III. iv. 175–78; III. vii. 196; III. viii. 201). In part IV, the utopian Houyhnhnms are equine Ancients, their society modelled on prestigious classical and Renaissance utopias, especially the society of Ancient Sparta, as described in Plutarch's *Life of Lycurgus* and approvingly mediated both by humanist writers in the early modern republican tradition and by several Royalist and Jacobite authors. While the satire's reactionary positives imply a conservative authorial position, the political attack is that of an extremist endorsing assassination and counter-revolution against usurpers. The combination of reaction and radicalism may be the signature of a crypto-Jacobite text. The restoration of 'the Liberty of *Old England*' was to be achieved through the destruction of 'Usurpation and Tyranny', as the openly Jacobite Duke of Wharton put it in a manifesto of 1726.[10] Swift's anti-Hanoverian political satire in *Gulliver's Travels* is artfully oblique and insinuated in a fictional narrative. The text that appeared in print in Swift's lifetime is also a castrated version of Swift's real menace. A passage intended for the end of chapter III in part III giving an account of the Lindalinian rebellion against the King of Laputa 'which had like to have put a Period to the Fate of that Monarchy, at least as it is now instituted' was suppressed. It is an ambiguous allegory of successful Irish resistance to King George's government. The passage concludes with Gulliver being assured that 'the Citizens were determined to fix it for ever, to kill the King and all his Servants, and entirely change the Government' (*PW* xi. 309–10). In part III, as printed, Caesar's assassin Marcus Brutus and his tyrannicide are given an excellent press – killing usurpers is clearly no murder – and Gulliver enjoys himself among the spirits in Glubbdubdrib 'beholding the Destroyers of Tyrants and Usurpers, and the Restorers of Liberty to oppressed and injured Nations' (III. vii. 196). This is as inflammatory as it reads, for approval of Brutus and the assassination of usurpers was appearing in openly seditious Jacobite verse and prose in King George's reign.[11]

Other, apparently apolitical, aspects of the satire also have resonance in contemporary Jacobite writing. For example, while ridicule of the law and of lawyers was a traditional satiric topos, Swift's animus is extreme and incendiary. Gulliver hopes that an effect of his book will be '*Smithfield* blazing with Pyramids of Law-Books' (*PW* xi. 6). In his account of the legal profession during his conversation with his Houyhnhnm master, Gulliver explains that *'Precedents'* are past unjust decisions produced by judges to justify 'the most iniquitous Opinions'. Gulliver emphasizes that judges are not interested in one's claim or title to property. The Houyhnhnm master learns that lawyers in modern Britain do not recognize hereditary title: 'they have wholly confounded the very Essence of Truth and Falshood, of Right and Wrong; so that it will take Thirty Years to decide whether the Field, left me by my Ancestors for six Generations, belong to me, or to a Stranger three Hundred Miles off.' Gulliver then immediately begins explaining the arbitrary way treason trials are conducted (IV. v. 249–50). It was a natural connection, for this satire on the legal system has resonance in contemporary Jacobite writing. It was a jibe of the *'Jacobites'* that 'the present Government is *Law-full'*. Indeed, many of the new laws in the expanding body of legislation in the Hanoverian state were directed against Jacobite treason. The Jacobites, of course, argued that the Hanoverian monarchy was an illegitimate usurpation without true hereditary title to the Crown. Ramsay concluded that if 'there is no difference between a lawful King and an Usurper, there is none betwixt a natural Heir and an unjust Possessor; betwixt a true Proprietor, and a Robber'. Jacobites claimed that all hereditary titles were really now in dispute. Deprivation of hereditary title leads to a society based on opinion and the Jacobite Matthias Earbery warned of 'the illimitable Tyranny of Opinion; for Opinion submits to no Laws . . . Opinion makes Precedents, and those Precedents are too often destructive of even Liberty itself'.[12] Swift's satire on law, and especially Gulliver's extreme claim that hereditary title in property is no longer recognized in law, would have had a subversive implication within the discursive context of dynastic political discourse. Much modern scholarship has been devoted to explaining the politics of *Gulliver's Travels.* What made the book appear seditious to many in Swift's first community of readers was the violence of the general satire and its particular topical application to the Hanoverian Whig government. The extremity of the attack seemed to suggest that the author was calling for the overthrow of the regime not its reform: that the intention was seditious and treasonable.

The putative author of the *Travels*, Lemuel Gulliver, is not reader friendly. The book begins with a prefatory 'Letter from Capt. Gulliver to his Cousin Sympson' in which an irate and misanthropic voice arraigns cousin, printer, and readers and harangues the 'human Species' (*PW* xi. 5–8). The book ends with the unbalanced putative author telling readers with any tincture of the vice of pride not to 'presume to appear in my Sight' (*PW* xi. 296). The final attack on pride is Swiftian, but the speaker is a proud ranting recluse in his 'little Garden at *Redriff*', horrified by his biological kinship with Yahoos and shunning his wife, family, and neighbours. Gulliver is a misanthrope in Timon's manner. The symptoms of Gulliver's kind of melancholy case were described by Robert Burton in *The Anatomy of Melancholy*:

> they delight in . . . desert places, to walk alone in . . . gardens . . . averse from company, as . . . Timon Misanthropus, they abhor all companions at last, even their nearest acquaintances and most familiar friends . . . confining themselves therefore wholly to their private houses or chambers . . . [they shun people for no reason, and hate them]'.[13]

However, Gulliver has not given up hope of a reconcilement with humankind and he is on medication. His first tentative steps towards rehabilitation are taken on his return to Europe, in Lisbon. He reports that he was able to walk in the street in the company of Captain Don Pedro Mendez 'but kept my Nose well stopped with Rue, or sometimes with Tobacco' (IV. xi. 288). Rue and tobacco were recommended as herbal cures for melancholy affliction in Burton's *The Anatomy of Melancholy*.[14] At the end of the book he reports that he is starting to have dinner with his wife again. But there is still a distance between them. Mimicking the Houyhnhnm master's treatment of himself (see IV. vii. 259), Gulliver permits her to sit 'at the farthest End of a long Table'. However, 'the Smell of a *Yahoo* continuing very offensive, I always keep my Nose well stopt with Rue, Lavender, or Tobacco-Leaves' (IV. xii. 295).[15]

In modern literary criticism much has been made of Gulliver's estrangement from humankind at the end. Gulliver is treated as a novelistic character and the misanthropy in the text identified as an expression of Gulliver's pathology rather than

Swift's ideology. It has been claimed that Gulliver is a brainwashed acolyte of the rational horses and in trying to emulate them he has become a madman. It is contended that Gulliver is gullible and wrong to have admired the Houyhnhnms, who are not a positive in the satire.[16] I share the view of many critics that this is reading against the grain of the text. Even if we try to view Gulliver as a psychologically credible character who has become mad, the text does not allow us to dismiss what he says so easily. Gulliver fears that in leaving Houyhnhnmland and returning to humankind he would relapse 'into my old Corruptions, for want of Examples to lead and keep me within the Paths of Virtue' (IV. x. 280, see also IV. vii. 258, IV. xi. 283). This is what we are invited to understand has happened to him. The recidivist Gulliver's absurd anti-social antics on his return to humankind primarily make Swift's misanthropic point that men and women are incapable of acting according to that Reason which is exemplified in the satire by the simple and sociable life of the Houyhnhnms. Gulliver who trots and whinnies like a horse can imitate the gait and voice of the Houyhnhnms but not their virtues. The self-righteous and proud Gulliver is an object of fun in the narrative, but his misanthropic conviction is confirmed by the book's excoriating satire on human society. Gulliver's conversion to Houyhnhnm views is presented in the text as an enlightenment that grew upon him by degrees rather than as a brainwashing. He is presented as convinced rather than credulous (IV. vii. 258, IV. x. 278). But, because he is incorrigibly human and proud, Gulliver is just unable to be reasonable. Swift's satiric insistence is that a rational animal would be what humans are not.

Gulliver's misanthropic stance, in fact, cannot simply be dismissed as the rant of a madman, for 'The Publisher to the Reader' gives Gulliver a good character reference. The Publisher reports that the author 'now lives retired, yet in good Esteem among his Neighbours'. It also seems that he has learned to imitate Houyhnhnm virtues as well as their trot, for the publisher reports that Gulliver does not say '*the Thing which is not*'. The Publisher informs the reader that 'the Author was so distinguished for his Veracity, that it became a Sort of Proverb among his Neighbours at *Redriff*, when any one affirmed a Thing, to say, it was as true as if Mr *Gulliver* had spoke it' (*PW* xi. 9). This is a Lucianic joke about the veracity of a lying traveller, but it is also an indication that Gulliver is a respectable figure in his community. And the book, after all, is supposed to have been prepared for the press after the voyage to Houyhnhnmland, but the first three voyages give no hint of Gulliver's disorientation or disillusionment. It is not, therefore, certain that Gulliver is necessarily supposed to be regarded as a madman who has not readjusted to society, though, even in the 'The Publisher to the Reader', a faint hint of puritan zealotry attaches itself to Lemuel (his biblical name means the 'chosen of God'). At the beginning of Gulliver's narrative we are told that he attended a Cambridge College of Puritan foundation and studied medicine at Leyden in the Netherlands, an educational destination abroad for Protestant Dissenters (I. i. 19). In the prefatory letter the Publisher tells the reader that he has observed 'Tombs and Monuments of the *Gullivers'* in *'Banbury'*, a town in Oxfordshire associated with Puritan fanaticism (PW xi. 9, as in the reference to 'a *Banbury Saint'* in Swift's *Mechanical Operation of the Spirit* (*PW* i. 184)). Other paratextual material contributes to the uncertainty. The frontispiece portraits of Gulliver in the 1726 and in the octavo 1735 editions of the *Travels* present the putative author to readers as a distinguished and authoritative rather than a deranged figure. But he is portrayed as an unkempt, possibly disturbed figure in the duodecimo edition of the *Travels* in 1735.[17]

In the letter to Pope about his 'Travells', Swift distanced himself from 'Timons manner' but not from the misanthropy. Swift was no misanthropic recluse – the range and depth of the friendships he inspired attest to that – but *Gulliver's Travels* is a misanthropic satire. Swift was careful that a book that might be and was regarded as impious and 'an insult on Providence, by depreciating the works of the Creator' (*Corr*. iii. 183), was associated with an unbalanced misanthropic sea captain and not the Dean of St Patrick's. The misanthropy provoked contemporary readers, such as Swift's first biographer the Fifth Earl of Orrery. But it pleased others who read the book as a response to latitudinarian Whig ideologues who 'consider men as reasoning creatures – as they should be, not as they are'.[18]

Swift, of course, is not Gulliver, but, in their misanthropic stance against the world, Swift and Gulliver are not as unlike as might at first be supposed or as Swift's rejection of Timon's manner in the letter to Pope would lead one to think. As in the frontispiece portraits of Jonathan Swift and Lemuel Gulliver that appear in the octavo edition of Swift's *Works* published by George Faulkner in 1735 (where Gulliver is Swift without the wig and wearing a raffish kerchief rather than a clerical collar), there are sometimes strong resemblances between the author and his fictional face.[19] Gulliver's extremism is an expression of a certain side of Swift. Behind Gulliver is the hidden face of Swift.

Like Gulliver, Swift is not reader friendly. The misanthropic Gulliver's statements in 'A Letter from Capt. Gulliver, to his Cousin Sympson' and at the end of his voyages are, in fact, fictional versions of Swift's comments in his correspondence about his intentions in the book. Gulliver expects his book to reform the world, with a deadline of 'seven Months' (*PW* xi. 6–7). Swift expects immediate conversion, telling Pope in his 1725 letter about the book's misanthropy: 'I never will have peace of mind till all honest men are of my Opinion: by Consequence you are to embrace it immediately and procure that all who deserve my Esteem may do so too. The matter is so clear that it will admit little dispute' (*CW* ii. 607). Gulliver declares to the 'gentle Reader' at the end of the book that 'my principal Design was to inform, and not to amuse thee' (IV. xii. 291). Swift tells Pope: 'the chief end I propose to my self in all my labors is to vex the world rather then divert it' (*CW* ii. 606). Gulliver is a hardline misanthropist claiming in 'A Letter from Capt. Gulliver, to his Cousin Sympson' that all humans are Yahoos and 'utterly incapable of Amendment by Precepts or Examples' (*PW* xi. 6). But this was also Swift's view expressed in a letter to Charles Ford: 'I think all men of wit should employ it in Satyr, if it will onely serve to vex Rogues, though it will not amend them. If my Talent that way were equal to the sourness of my temper I would write nothing else' (*Corr.* iv. 138). He tells Thomas Sheridan to 'expect no more from Man than such an Animal is capable of, and you will every day find my Description of Yaho[o]s more resembling' (*CW* ii. 595). Swift calls people Yahoos, as in his satiric poem 'The Yahoo's

Overthrow' (*Poems*, 539–41). The Houyhnhnm master says that, 'although he hated the *Yahoos* of this Country, yet he no more blamed them for their odious Qualities, than he did a *Gnnayh* (a Bird of Prey) for its Cruelty' (IV. v. 248). Swift told Pope that after all he did 'not hate Mankind' because he did not regard humans as 'reasonable Animals'. He uses the analogy of (the Prime Minister as) a bird of prey: 'I am no more angry with [Walpole] th[a]n I was with the Kite that last week flew away with one of my Chickins and yet I was pleas'd when one of my Servants shot him two days after' (*CW* ii. 623). The Houyhnhnms debate whether the humanoid Yahoos 'should be exterminated from the Face of the Earth' (*PW* xi. 271), an echo of Genesis 6: 7, where God says: 'I will destroy man whom I have created from the face of the earth.' The final judgement is presaged in the *Travels*, especially in the King of Brobdingnag's observation to Gulliver: 'I cannot but conclude the Bulk of your Natives, to be the most pernicious Race of little odious Vermin that Nature ever suffered to crawl upon the Surface of the Earth' (II. vi. 132). The Houyhnhnm extermination proposal, and the King of Brobdingnag's senti-ments on Gulliver's countrymen and horror when Gulliver tells him of gunpowder war, might be compared with Apollo's reaction to human wickedness and the art of war in the contemporary Tory version of Boccalini's *Advertisements from Parnassus* (1704): 'Since Men were grown so wretchedly Foolish and Wicked . . . He desired . . . to rid the World of such Vermin . . . That a second Deluge might at once sweep 'em off the Face of the Earth.'[20] The Houyhnhnm proposal and the King of Brobdingnag's words reflect Swift's own rhetorical extremism and that of some contemporary Tory satirists and pamphlet-eers. In alluding to the Biblical Flood by echoing Genesis 6: 7, Swift invokes divine punitive fury against offending human-kind. Lemuel Gulliver is the chosen one who builds a boat and escapes the fate projected for Yahoos and his book is intended to effect the moral regeneration of European Yahoos. In allowing Gulliver to get away, the Houyhnhnms in fact reflect a characteristic of God's exterminations in Genesis and in other Books of the Bible. He does not utterly destroy all 'from off the face of the earth' (Amos 9: 8).[21] But the principal effect of the misanthropic extremism at the end of the *Travels* is a cold-blooded conviction that humans are Yahoos and too depraved to be saved.

Swift wrote to Pope on 29 September 1725, referring to their friend John Arbuthnot: 'O, if the World had but a dozen Arbuthnotts in it I would burn my Travells' (*CW* ii. 607). Similarly, the speaker in Lord Rochester's 'A Satyre against Reason and Mankind' claims he will recant his misanthropy if a just, good man of right reason could be produced. Hardcore misanthropic satirists do not want to appear unreasonable to readers and will court common sense if strategic concessions to humanity might persuade readers. Swift did not burn his book nor did he recant his misanthropy. There would not be a dozen good humans in *Gulliver's Travels*, but the satirist is willing to concede that there might be some decent people, gaudily good exceptions that tend to prove the general rule. The Portuguese Captain Don Pedro de Mendez who preserves Gulliver and counsels him in part IV, and other good characters such as Lord Munodi in part III, and Glumdalclitch and the King of Brobdingnag in part II, function in this way.

Importantly, these four exceptional characters are also precise embodiments of Swiftian positives. Interestingly, Swift had Portuguese cousins (*Corr.* v. 58). The friendly and benevolent, but rather austere bachelor Don Pedro, a human version of Gulliver's Houyhnhnm master, treats Gulliver as if he was a near family relation. This good Roman Catholic Gulliver meets on the high seas is also clearly to be contrasted with the perfidious anti-Christian Dutchman of part III. The disaffected Lord Munodi in part III embodies the conservative reaction of the text's politics in his admirable old-fashioned stance against the ruinous innovations being imposed by the arbitrary Laputan court. In part II Glumdalclitch is a brave and an affectionate companion and nurse to Gulliver, qualities valued in Swift's birthday poems to Stella. The good giant King of Brobdingnag articulates Opposition political views in a damning critique of Gulliver's England. The King's comments in his conversation with Gulliver on England's taxes, national debt, extensive wars, foreign deployment of the fleet, and a mercenary standing army (see II. vi. 130–1) were recognized by contemporary readers as 'a common *Jacobite* Insinuation'.[22] There has been much speculation about whom the King of

Brobdingnag suggests or if he is meant to signify anyone in particular. The contemporary 'King' he may have insinuated was the exiled Stuart Pretender, 'James III'. The Pretender had appeared as 'a huge Giant' across the sea in a political allegory printed in Dublin in 1714 by Daniel Tompson (who published works by Swift and his High Tory friend Thomas Sheridan). The allegory defended Swift's friend Sir Constantine Phipps, the High Church Tory, crypto-Jacobite Lord Chancellor of Ireland in Queen Anne's last administration.[23] The Jacobite Duke of Wharton's description of the Stuart Pretender and account of his interview with him (in which the King points out to Wharton the flagitious corruption of the government in England), published in 1726, has some striking similarities, including verbal echoes, with Gulliver's account of his meeting with the King of Brobdingnag in part II and with Brutus in part III.[24] A copy of *Gulliver's Travels* was sent to the exiled Stuart King.[25] The King of Brobdingnag is the fictional embodiment of the dynastic challenge that Swift's Opposition politics potentially posed to the Hanoverian Whig establishment, whether or not Swift really was a Jacobite.

While there are significant exceptions to the general misanthropy, Gulliver's misanthropic stance against the world at the end is like Swift in some moods. Gulliver's reasons for not wanting to return to Europe after he departs from Houyhnhnmland have interesting resonances in Swift's correspondence and biography. Gulliver does not want to return 'to live in the Society and under the Government of *Yahoos*'. He would choose 'rather to trust my self among these *Barbarians* [the 'Savages' of 'New-Holland'], than live with *European Yahoos*' (IV. xi. 283–5). Swift told Charles Wogan in 1736 that he had 'become an obscure exile in a most obscure and enslaved country' and that 'I would prefer living among the Hottentots, if it were in my power' than under the reigning party government (*Corr*. iv. 468). Considering arbitrary government in *The Sentiments of a Church-of-England Man* (written in 1708), Swift writes that 'a *Savage* is in a happier State of Life, than a *Slave* at the Oar' (*PW* ii. 15). In Lisbon Gulliver does not want his account of the Houyhnhnms made known, 'because the least Hint of such a Story would . . . probably put me in Danger of being imprisoned, or burnt by the *Inquistion*' (IV. xi. 288).

Swift should know. *A Tale of a Tub* was placed on the Vatican's *Index* and Swift was assured that 'the *Inquisition* in *Portugal* was pleased to burn [Isaac Bickerstaff's *Predictions for the Year 1708*], and condemn the Author and Readers of them' (*PW* ii. 160). Gulliver's fears here are also a parody of William Dampier's fears about the Portuguese '*Inquisition*' in Brazil: 'if they got me into their Clutches (and it seems, when I was last ashore they had narrowly watch'd me) the Governor himself could not release me. Besides I might either be murther'd in the Streets . . . or Poysoned, if I came ashore any more.'[26] As for Gulliver's preference for horses and the stable to the world of Yahoos at the end of his Travels, well, Swift's correspondence attests to his own fondness for horses. Amusingly, Swift told Henrietta Howard, the Countess of Suffolk and mistress of George II, of the following domestic misfortune. Swift was ironically willing to face the world as Gulliver:

> I will tell you an odd Accident, that this night, while I was caressing one of my Houyhnhnms, he bit my little finger so cruelly, that I am hardly able to write, and I impute the Cause to some fore-knowledge in him, that I was going to write to a Sieve Yahoo (for so you are pleased to call yourself) . . . (1 Feb. 1727, *Corr.* iii. 196)

Swift joked about, and his friends and enemies responded to, the outré pornographic aspect of the misanthropic comedy in *Gulliver's Travels*. The work is something of an eighteenth-century bestiality site. In Brobdingnag, Gulliver is used as a sex toy by the giant Maids of Honour: 'The handsomest among these Maids of Honour, a pleasant frolicksome Girl of sixteen, would sometimes set me astride upon one of her Nipples; with many other Tricks, wherein the Reader will excuse me for not being over particular' (II. v. 119). However, there was also a 'frolicksome Animal', a monkey, which peeps in at Gulliver, who is in his room or box. The monkey abducts Gulliver, holding him 'as a Nurse doth a Child she is going to suckle'. The monkey, Gulliver believes, 'took me for a young one of his own Species, by his often stroaking my Face very gently with his other Paw'. Gulliver is nursed by the monkey like a baby until eventually rescued (II. v. 121–3). In Houyhnhnmland, Gulliver regards the Yahoos as odious beasts. However, a young female Yahoo attempts to copulate with the naked Gulliver in a stream (IV. viii. 266–7). This incident is usually understood in literary criticism as evoking the scenario of European–Native sexual encounter (though with the native female as the sexual predator in this contact). The spectacle, however, is primarily one of bestiality. The misanthropic point of the episode is that Gulliver is forced to recognize his biological kinship with brutality: 'I could no longer deny, that I was a real *Yahoo* ... since the Females had a natural Propensity to me as one of their own Species.' The 'Brute' was a brunette not a redhead, Gulliver reflects, so there was no excuse for this cross-species sexual passion, 'for an Appetite a little irregular'. We are also dealing with underage bestiality: 'her Countenance did not make an Appearance altogether so hideous as the rest of the Kind; for, I think, she could not be above Eleven Years old' (IV. viii. 267). Of course, Gulliver by this point in the narrative has shown a preference for horses. At the end of the *Travels* Gulliver reports that he is spending at least four hours every day in his stable speaking to his stallions (IV. xi. 290). Whereas Swift's first biographer and many later readers have been disgusted by the misanthropy and the breaches of decorum in part IV, Swift's friends and enemies responded creatively. The fourth of Pope's amusing verses on *Gulliver's Travels*, 'Mary Gulliver to Captain Lemuel Gulliver', printed in the 1735 Faulkner edition of the work, is a neglected wife's lament for her estranged husband and his preference for sleeping in the stable with the sorrel mare.[27] The Whig Lady Mary Wortley Montagu ignored the satire and focused on the quasi-pornographic, transgressive comedy in *Gulliver's Travels*, diagnosing a Tory Scriblerian group sexual pathology:

> Great Eloquence have they employ'd to prove themselves Beasts, and show such a veneration for Horses, that since the Essex Quaker no body has appear'd so passionately devoted to that species; and to say truth, they talk of a stable with so much warmth and Affection I can't help suspecting some very powerfull Motive at the bottom of it.[28]

Gulliver's Travels is a general satire in the vehicle of a mock-travel book. The work is not a novel, although it is often regarded as such. The putative author Gulliver is much more a device or cipher for the satirist than a credible, psychologically consistent or developing novelistic character with depth or interiority, as several critics have shown. The perfunctory opening three paragraphs in which Gulliver gives *'some Account of himself'* display Swift's lack of interest in developing character and indeed parody the interest in character shown in contemporary first-person narratives. Gulliver is given the rudimentary verisimilitude necessary for him to be functional in the narrative. He is an ordinary Englishman, the middle son of a Midlands family. His education, Cambridge and Leyden, suggests a man of Whiggish disposition well affected to the establishment. Gulliver has, however, two extraordinary and very convenient traits: a violent desire to travel and a great facility in learning languages. When the reader, unusually, is given what appears to be a glimpse of Gulliver's inner life, the context is ridiculous and Swift's mode is mock-pathos. Gulliver in Brobdingnag reports one of his *'Adventures'*: 'I likewise broke my right Shin against the Shell of a Snail, which I happened to stumble over, as I was walking alone, and thinking on poor *England'* (II. v. 117–18).[29] When Gulliver confides to the reader about his formative years with 'Mr. *Bates'*, 'my good Master Mr. *Bates'*, '*Mr. Bates*, my Master', and, finally, his 'good Master *Bates'*, his brief autobiographical revelation of himself as a developing character is derided as an unseemly self-absorption. The novelistic interest in character is a textual self-abuse (I. i. 19–20). Swift uses Gulliver to satirize the egoism of first-person voyage narratives and the circumstantiality of their authors. Gulliver outdoes them all in over-particularity. An extended circumstantial account of how he arranges to defecate in Lilliput is described as an 'Adventure' (I. ii. 29–30), as is an account of how his hat was transported across Lilliput (I. iii. 41–2). Amusingly, Swift's over-particular voyager abruptly terminates a highly particular account of his adventures as a sexual toy among the Brobdingnagian maids of honour: 'the Reader will excuse me for not being over particular' (II. v. 119). In part IV, however, Gulliver ends an account of his diet in Houyhnhnmland with the recognition that he is really only a cipher and that readers are interested in things other than the central character: 'THIS is enough to say upon the Subject of my Dyet, where-with other Travellers fill their Books, as if the Readers were personally concerned, whether we fare well or ill' (IV. ii. 232–3).

The principal interest of a satire like *Gulliver's Travels* is in the point being made about the world outside the text not in the 'character' or 'persona' through which it is made. Swift's political satire, for example, consistently condemns tyranny and arbitrary power, but Gulliver, through whom the satire is articulated, lacks consistency on the subject. In part I, Gulliver, through a naval stratagem and without loss of life, creates the conditions for a peace between the empires of Lilliput and Blefuscu, but the Emperor of Lilliput wants to impose his arbitrary will over Blefuscu and its people. Gulliver refuses to gratify the Emperor's wishes, protesting that he 'would never be an Instrument of bringing a free and brave People into Slavery' (I. v. 53). But in part II, Gulliver 'hopes to ingratiate my self farther into his Majesty's Favour' by offering the King of Brobdingnag the secret of gunpowder war, which 'would have made him absolute Master of the Lives, the Liberties, and the Fortunes of his People'. The good King rejects with horror Gulliver's proposal for crimes against humanity (II. vii. 134–5). There is ideological consistency in the satire on arbitrary power, but Gulliver is clearly manipulated to serve the satirist's immediate ends. The satiric animus against the Dutch in part III of *Gulliver's Travels* is not an expression of Gulliver's 'character'. Gulliver studied at Leyden (I. i. 19), but we are not being invited to suppose that Gulliver must have had some unspecified bad experience there in his youth that leads to his dislike of them. The satire's imputation of the anti-Christian and anti-English conduct of the Dutch in the East Indies and Japan (III. i. 154–5, III. xi. 216–17) is a reprise of Swift's Tory propaganda against the Dutch as England's real enemies. The point of the satire is to discredit the Dutch and encourage antipathy for them. For Swift, the Dutch were Britain's treacherous allies and predatory commercial rivals, the international face of Calvinism, and, by the terms of the Barrier Treaty (1709), made by the Whigs and obnoxious to Swift, the military support of the Hanoverian succession in Britain.

Similarly, in the famous attack on colonialism delivered by Gulliver at the end of the *Travels*, Gulliver excepts Britain from the denunciation: 'this Description, I confess, doth by no means affect the *British* Nation, who may be an Example to the whole World for their Wisdom, Care, and Justice in planting Colonies' (IV. xii. 294). The obvious point of the sardonic irony is that Britain is as flagitious as other European nations. Swift is in fact parodying contemporary Whig-speak asserting the exceptionalism of 'his Majesty's Dominions' when it comes to planting colonies. The loyal Whig journal *Cato's Letters* found English liberty exemplified in Britain's productive American slave plantations: 'the English planters in America, besides maintaining themselves and ten times as many Negroes, maintain likewise great numbers of their countrymen in England. Such are the blessings of liberty, and such is the difference which it makes between country and country!'[30] The effect of the whole passage on European colonies in part IV, chapter XII, is a sweeping condemnation of colonialism. The interest is not in whether or not Gulliver is sincere, inconsistent, sarcastic, or cautious when he excepts Britain from the denunciation. As Claude Rawson has argued of the satiric onslaught on colonialism: 'the electric fact is the onslaught, not the nature of the speaker . . . if you really want to stay more or less on the rails you must concentrate on the point being made, not on who is making it'.[31] Characterization is inconsistent throughout the book and is always subordinate to immediate satiric purpose. The Laputans are hopelessly abstracted impractical philosophers when Swift is satirizing pure science. They are calculating tyrants when Swift is satirizing arbitrary courts. The Yahoos are sometimes regarded as an animal species and beasts of burden; at other times they are to be understood as degenerate humans. The Houyhhnms are sometimes obtuse or 'ignorant'; at other times they are wise and acute, as required for Swift's local satiric effect.

Gulliver is the cipher for Swift's hard-core misanthropy in part IV. Gulliver experiences a simple and tranquil life of reason and becomes a proselyte for it. The problem for Gulliver and his readers is that the rational life, lacking in vicious variety, is what human life is not, as one of Swift's famous satiric lists emphatically declares. Gulliver describes his *'happy Life among the* Houyhnhnms':

I enjoyed perfect Health of Body, and Tranquility of Mind; I did not feel the Treachery or Inconstancy of a Friend, nor the Injuries of a secret or open Enemy. I had no Occasion of bribing, flattering or pimping, to procure the Favour of any great Man, or of his Minion. I wanted no Fence against Fraud or Oppression: Here was neither Physician to destroy my Body, nor Lawyer to ruin my Fortune: No Informer to watch my Words and Actions, or forge Accusations against me for Hire: Here were no Gibers, Censurers, Backbiters, Pick-pockets, Highwaymen, House-breakers, Attorneys, Bawds, Buffoons, Gamesters, Politicians, Wits, Spleneticks, tedious Talkers, Controvertists, Ravishers, Murderers, Robbers, Virtuoso's; no Leaders or Followers of Party and Faction; no Encouragers to Vice, by Seducement or Examples: No Dungeon, Axes, Gibbets, Whipping-posts, or Pillories; No cheating Shop-keepers or Mechanicks: No Pride, Vanity or Affectation: No Fops, Bullies, Drunkards, strolling Whores, or Poxes: No ranting, lewd, expensive Wives: No stupid, proud Pedants: No importunate, over-bearing, quarrelsome, noisy, roaring, empty, conceited, swearing Companions: No Scoundrels raised from the Dust upon the Merit of their Vices; nor Nobility thrown into it on account of their Virtues: No Lords, Fidlers, Judges or Dancing-masters.   (IV. x. 276–7)

Gulliver has come to hate himself and his kind, but he finds it impossible to be a Houyhnhnm because, in a Swiftian subversion of a traditional definition of man, man is not a rational animal. Like the satirists Samuel Butler, the Earl of Rochester, and Tom Brown before him, Swift focused on that definition of man found in logic texts of the seventeenth century: that 'man was a rational animal'. The proposition was demonstrated by contrasting the horse as an example of the non-rational animal. The logical commonplace is alluded to in one of Swift's favourite works, Samuel Butler's satire *Hudibras*. Sir Hudibras 'was in *Logick* a great Critick, | Profoundly skill'd in Analytick' who would 'undertake to prove by force | Of Argument, a Man's no Horse'. Rochester's misanthropic satire 'Tunbridge Wells' concludes by preferring the horse as 'the wiser Creature'. If the speaker of Rochester's 'A Satyre against Reason and Mankind' had freedom to choose, he would be any creature 'but that vain Animal | Who is so proud of being Rational'. Swift invents a satiric fable that strikingly inverts the familiar definition. Part IV sets out to prove a man is no horse, but with a stinging insult in the tail, for in Swift's provocative reversal horses are the rational animals and humankind worse than irrational brutality. As Swift told Pope in a letter about his intentions in *Gulliver's Travels* on 29 September 1725: 'I have got Materials Towards a Treatis proving the falsity of that Definition animal rationale, and to show it should be only *rationis capax*' (*CW* ii. 607).[32] Gulliver informs us that the 'Word *Houyhnhnm*, in their Tongue, signifies a *Horse*; and its Etymology, *the Perfection of Nature*' (IV. iii. 235). The Houyhnhnms are presented as self-identical with nature. A naturalistic argument against the venerable belief that Man was the most perfect creature in nature was advanced in *The Circe of Signior Giovanni Battista Gelli*. Tom Brown's 1702 version of the sixteenth-century Florentine's work, especially the seventh dialogue concerning horse versus man, was one of Swift's probable sources for part IV.[33] The Houyhnhnms are an image of the rational animal humans claim to be but are not. This non-human Houyhnhnm order is by definition unattainable for humankind; it is nevertheless the utopian expression of the ideological programme of the satire. While the mythic Houyhnhnms are horses not humans, the homonymous similarity between 'Houyhnhnm' and 'human' and the fact that the order of the Houyhnhnms is modelled on classical utopias enable readers to understand them as pre-Christian 'Ancients' or utopians. These equine arcadian Ancients have an oral culture and are authoritarian, communistic, agrarian, pacifist, ascetic, and, of course, vegetarian and nudist. What modern readers have regarded as the negative aspects or limitations of the Houyhnhnms in fact starkly express the apparent positives of this satire or embody Swift's didactic positions and personal longings expressed in other writings. A few examples must suffice. The following points have been made many times before, but are worth reiterating, since the view that the Houyhnhnms are not endorsed by Swift's text has a powerful hold in modern literary criticism, and has led, in my view, to a sweetening and softening of what really is an unpalatable, hardline extremist text.

It is often claimed that the Houyhnhnms are cold and passionless. Their austerity, however, is a sign of moral virtue in the fable. We are told that the Houyhnhnm language 'expressed the Passions very well', although 'their Language doth not abound in Variety of Words, because their Wants and Passions are fewer than among us' (IV. i. 226; IV. iv. 242). They are not without feelings. They exhibit friendliness, civility, and even delight (IV. iii. 235) in their contact and conversation with Gulliver. The Houyhnhnm master even becomes awkwardly 'human' for Gulliver's sake: Houyhnhnms are not supposed to lie, but the Houyhnhnm master conceals the truth about Gulliver wearing clothes when Gulliver asks him to do so (IV. iii. 237). He also withholds the whole truth when he puts off telling Gulliver the bad news that he is to be deported from Houyhnhnmland (IV. ix. 273). Gulliver is viewed as a corrupting influence by the Houyhnhnms in the Assembly, and the text, in showing the effect he seems to be having on his Houyhnhnm master, supports their unsentimental view of him. Gulliver's expulsion from Houyhnhnmland is meant to reflect badly on Gulliver and humankind, not on the Houyhnhnm Assembly that delivers the 'Exhortation' for his removal (IV. x. 279–80). Swift's insulting point is that there is no place for humans in a rational natural order. The Houyhnhnm Assembly's fear that Gulliver might lead a Yahoo insurrection and 'destroy the *Houyhnhnms* cattle' is not unreasonable, given what Gulliver has told them human nature is capable of (IV. x. 279). Indeed, the Houyhnhnm view of Gulliver as potential cattle-killer is anticipated in the text. Upon his arrival in Houyhnhnmland, Gulliver struck a Yahoo: 'I drew my Hanger, and gave him a good Blow with the flat Side of it; for I durst not strike him with the Edge, fearing the Inhabitants might be provoked against me, if they should come to know, that I had killed or maimed any of their Cattle' (IV. i. 224). Gulliver, who enters Houyhnhnmland in 1711, is imaged as a savage Irish hougher (Swift is probably recalling accounts of 'Houghers of Cattle' in Irish counties in 1711 and 1712 (see *PW* xvi. 525; *CW* i. 420)). The reader is not unprepared for the Houyhnhnm Assembly's later hardline attitude.

The Houyhnhnms do not publicly express grief. But this does not mean they do not have feelings. There is perhaps a subtle suggestion that the stoic Houyhnhnm wife who is late keeping an appointment because her husband had died that morning, and who conducts herself as if nothing had happened, later dies of a broken heart (IV. ix. 274–5). Perhaps Swift wished he could have this outward emotional calm. He seems to have made no public display of his very real grief at the death of Esther Johnson, wanting to be left alone and not attending the funeral (*PW* v. 227, 229). Gulliver's passionate desire for long life is satirized in the Struldbrug episode in part III of *Gulliver's Travels* (III. x. 207–14), as is his public display of grief and despair in falling into a 'Swoon' when told he must leave Houyhnhnmland (IV. x. 280). I think that a passionate man, who felt deeply or experienced the traumas of love, guilt, and betrayal, might well fantasize about a world of tranquillity, and an ontology free from such emotions or indifferent to them, a state embodied by Swift in the mythic horses. The final scene in Houyhnhnmland, in which the Houyhnhnm master and his friends bid farewell to Gulliver as he sails away is one of restrained pathos. The servant Sorrel Nag's affection for Gulliver is mentioned in a parenthetical undertone: 'I often heard the Sorrel Nag (who always loved me) crying out . . . Take Care of thy self, gentle *Yahoo*' (IV. xi. 283). They may be outwardly unemotional, but the Houyhnhnms are certainly not passionless. It is explicitly stated and shown, for instance, that they hate the Yahoos.

So-called Houyhnhnm limitations, their ignorance of the 'art of war' and of astronomy, for instance, are clearly positives in a book that satirizes militarism throughout and that ridicules the astronomical speculations and fears of the Laputans. Similarly the fact that the Houyhnhnms have only an oral literary tradition is a sign of an ideal utopian society in a satire where book production is characteristic of corrupt societies like Lilliput, and 'the least corrupted', the Brobdingnagians, have libraries that are not very large. Houyhnhnm society presents in absolute form what the satire elsewhere affirms as positive. Notoriously, the Houyhnhnms are said to be without difference of opinion (IV. viii. 267; IV. x. 277). Their debate about whether to exterminate the Yahoos or inflict genocide in a generation is as close as they get to a difference in opinion (IV. ix. 271–3). Yet it is difference of opinion and dissent that Swift's satire identifies as the radical human problem. 'Difference in Opinions' has 'cost many Millions of Lives' (IV. v. 246). The Laputans in part III are satirized for 'passionately disputing

77

every Inch of a Party Opinion' (III. ii. 164). Outward public conformity in Church and State is the ideal of good government in Swift's satire (I. vi. 60; II. vi. 131). The logic of the satire is that the uniformity of the Houyhnhnms is something readers are supposed to admire.

There is also little doubt that the Houyhnhnms are embodiments of Swiftian ideals and longings documented elsewhere. The Houyhnhnms have 'no Fondness for their Colts or Foles' (IV. viii. 268) and their manner of education is a reprise of the public education system in uncorrupted Lilliput, where parental involvement, affection, and 'any fondling Expressions' are not permitted (I. vi. 61). More than twenty years before he wrote *Gulliver's Travels*, Swift wrote down as one of his resolutions 'When I come to be old': 'Not to be fond of Children, or let them come near me hardly' (*PW* i, p. xxxvii). The Houyhnhnms marry for eugenic reasons 'not upon the Account of *Love'*. 'Courtship, Love, Presents, Joyntures, Settlements, have no Place in their Thoughts; or Terms whereby to express them in their Language. The young Couple meet and are joined, merely because it is the Determination of their Parents and Friends' (IV. viii. 268–9). Swift expressed similar views in *A Letter to a Young Lady, on her Marriage*, written in 1723 when he was also at work on *Gulliver*, praising 'a Match of Prudence, and common Good-liking, without any Mixture of that ridiculous Passion which hath no Being, but in Play-Books and Romances' (*PW* ix. 89).

If the Houyhnhnm polity is the satire's ideal, it raises disturbing questions about the relation of *Gulliver's Travels* to the slaving society in which it was produced, for the Houyhnhnm treatment of the humanoid Yahoos is analogous to slavery. There is ambivalence in the textual record of Swift's attitude to slavery. One of the cruellest ironies in Swift's work occurs in *The History of the Four Last Years of the Queen*, his history of Queen Anne's Tory government of 1710–14, which had negotiated the peace with France. Swift recorded the fifth article of the *'Preliminary Demands for* Great Britain' in the Peace Treaty as follows:

> The Assiento (or Liberty of selling Negroes to the *Spanish* West-Indies) to be granted to the *English*, in as full a manner as the

French possess it at present; And such Places in the said *West-Indies* to be assigned to the Persons concerned in this Trade, for the Refreshment and Sale of their Negroes, as shall be found necessary and convenient.   (*PW* vii. 48)

The 'Liberty' to be gained by England in the Treaty of Utrecht is placed by Swift in parentheses, graphically shadowed, as if what the Assiento is can only be spoken in undertone. (In Queen Anne's Speech to Parliament of 6 June 1712, reproduced by Swift in his *History*, the traffic in African slaves is no longer explained as a 'Liberty'. The Queen told Parliament: ' "BUT the Part which we have borne in the Prosecution of this War entitling us to some Distinction in the Terms of Peace, I have insisted, and obtained, that the Assiento, or Contract for furnishing the *Spanish West-Indies* with Negroes, shall be made with us for the Term of thirty Years, in the same Manner as it has been enjoyed by the *French* for ten Years past" ' (*PW* vii. 132)). If the parentheses in Swift's account of the Assiento article and the omission of the word 'Liberty' in the Queen's Speech betray any recognition of an obscene irony in describing the traffic in slaves as a British liberty, it is not in evidence elsewhere in the work, where Swift writes that it will make 'an odd Sound in History, and appear hardly Credible' that the Dutch could even debate whether 'the Queen of *Great Britain* ... should be suffered to enjoy after a Peace the Liberty granted Her by *Spain* of selling *African* Slaves in the *Spanish* Dominions of *America*' (*PW* vii. 123–4). Swift records the government's insistence during the peace negotiations that Britain acquire exclusive rights to 'the Assiento for Negroes'. The Lord Treasurer 'would rather lose his Head' than share the trade (*PW* vii. 109; and see 119, 120). The distance between Swift's apparent attitude to the slave trade and that of the 'Modest Proposer' for whom slavery is just a matter of economic calculation (see *PW* xii. 111) may not be so great as modern readers might at first suppose.

While anti-slavery sentiment and argument were expressed in the public domain and across the political and confessional spectrum in Swift's time, an euphemistic avoidance of the subject of colonial slavery and the transatlantic slave trade, rather than ignorance of it, seems characteristic of much early eighteenth-century writing.[34] *Gulliver's Travels* reflects the linguistic habit of silence, occlusion, and euphemism on the subject of the slave trade. Gulliver is circumspect about his earlier voyages and profits: 'I was Surgeon successively in two Ships, and made several Voyages, for six Years, to the *East* and *West-Indies*; by which I got some Addition to my Fortune' (I. i. 20). For contemporaries this would have implied that he had involvement in the slaving voyages of the South Sea Company. Gulliver is typically vague about the nature of his economic enterprises and goods.[35] A surgeon on South Sea Company ships to the sugar plantations in the West Indies had the physical selection of slaves as one of his principal responsibilities. Gulliver's various disasters on his four commercial voyages and especially his misfortunes in the South Seas voyages had resonance for contemporaries as symbolic of the financial crash of 1720 known as the South Sea Bubble in which the South Sea Company, which held the Assiento, had criminally inflated its stock value. Gulliver's own repeated captivity would also have had resonance for contemporaries, as capture and enslavement were the fate of large numbers of European mariners in Swift's time. Gulliver, of course, is an agent of his trading and slaving society, but Swift's satire explicitly excoriates the practices of colonial slavery (IV. xii. 294). After denouncing colonialism, Gulliver reports that 'those Countries which I have described do not appear to have a Desire of being conquered, and enslaved, murdered or driven out by Colonies; nor abound either in Gold, Silver, Sugar or Tobacco' – the commodities associated with European colonialism and the slave trade in the New World (IV. xii. 295).

Yet the book is ambivalent about the institution of slavery. Houyhnhnmland is modelled on the caste and slave societies found in classical utopias. Houyhnhnm treatment of the Yahoos recalls Ancient Sparta's treatment of the helots, a serf class with pariah status who were periodically slaughtered, as recorded by Thucydides and Plutarch.[36] Swift's Houyhnhnms do not practise some of the customs of Ancient Sparta that were incompatible with Christian morality: the practice of theft and the wife sharing for eugenic purposes in Lycurgan Sparta, for example, are modified in Houyhnhnmland. There is no private property in Houyhnhnmland, and the Houyhnhnms have the institution of marriage and practise child (rather than wife) sharing. However, Swift retains the violent Spartan solution of slaughtering helots when the Houyhnhnms, who have already destroyed one generation of Yahoos, debate the expediency of exterminating them all 'from the Face of the Earth' (IV. ix. 271). The echo of Genesis, in fact, conflates the violence of the admired Ancient Spartans in dealing with their troublesome helots with the righteous fury of God against sinful humankind. And, although Gulliver denounces colonialism, he would accept a reverse colonialism. Instead of 'conquering that magnanimous Nation', Gulliver wishes sufficient Houyhnhnms could be sent from the South Seas in order to civilize Europe with their virtues (IV. xii. 293–4). Swift's '*Houyhnhnms* and *Yahoos* have no more Existence than the Inhabitants of *Utopia*' (*PW* xi. 8), but the fiction was a stalking horse for a satirist with extreme, even unspeakable, things to say.

5

Poems

'I have been only a Man of Rhimes,' Swift wrote in 1732, 'and that upon Trifles, never having written serious Couplets in my Life; yet never any without a moral View' (*Corr.* iv. 52). Swift began and ended his literary career writing poetry and produced as substantial a corpus of work as Alexander Pope. Swift's pungent, deflationary, irreverent satire found its natural expression in the four-beat measure of the tetrameter couplet. In the twentieth century, the editions of Harold Williams and Pat Rogers, and the criticism of Claude Rawson among many others, have confirmed Swift's canonical status as the major poet that poets like Lord Byron always thought he was.

Swift is an innovatory practitioner in a number of poetic genres: pindaric odes, town eclogues, satiric colloquial light verse, elegies and obituaries, libel and lampoon. He is notorious, of course, for his so-called scatological or excremental verse, but even these poems are significant innovations in an existing tradition of Juvenalian anti-feminist verse whose practitioners included Joseph Hall, John Oldham, Robert Gould, and Tom Brown among many others. Swift's scatological poems have wider satiric range than many contemporary anti-feminist satires, characteristically containing multiple targets. There is violent animus against the female body figured as corrupt in these poems, but the male body and certainly the extravagant idealism of male lovers are accorded searing attention also, as are those poetic forms of idealism, amatory and pastoral verse. Swift's scatological poems, incongruously enough, advance an idiosyncratic case for cosmetics, and are highly ironic, unillusioned instances of an under-noticed High

Church Anglican body of writing in defence of the use of cosmetics, as will be identified here.

The great satiric genre in poetry is formal verse satire, which in English refers to poems based on Roman classical satires by Horace (65–8 BCE), Persius (AD 34–62), and Juvenal (*c.* AD 60–148). Juvenal provided a model of outspoken, righteous indignation at vice for English verse satire. Swift's famous epitaph (*PW* xiii. 149) speaks of his 'savage indignation' and Swift is often regarded as the Juvenal of literature in English. Although Juvenalian rage is palpable in Swift's satiric poems, he eschewed the elevated tone of denunciation associated with the Roman satirist and preferred a more downbeat and familiar style of ridicule and raillery. 'I the lofty style decline,' he accurately said of his satiric manner in 'To a Lady. Who Desired the Author to Write Some Verses upon her in the Heroic Style' (l. 230, in *Poems*, 520; see also ll. 49–52, 143–8, in *Poems*, 516, 518).[1] Formal verse satire is ostensibly reformative; it prosecutes vice and prescribes virtue. In 'To a Lady', for example, Swift pays lip service to satire's reformative end as his political satire exposes and punishes the corrupt monarch and politician:

> I, who love to have a fling,
> Both at senate house and king;
> That they might some better way tread,
> To avoid the public hatred;
> Thought no method more commodious,
> Than to show their vices odious:
> Which I chose to make appear,
> Not by anger, but a sneer:
> As my method of reforming
> Is by laughing, not by storming
>
> (ll. 233–42, in *Poems*, 520)

The problem is that the poem complains that neither court nor parliament nor public ever mend (ll. 50–6) and the poem seems much more interested in performing the punishment than reforming the victim. The poem's intimate violence displays the quasi-pornographic fervour of a pedagogue punishing the posteriors of schoolboys. Swift leaves political reformation to other Opposition writers; he prefers the role of a dominatrix:

If I can but fill my niche,
I attempt no higher pitch.
Leave to D'Anvers and his mate,
Maxims wise to rule the state.
Pulteney deep, accomplished St Johns,
Scourge the villains with a vengeance:
Let me, though the smell be noisome,
Strip their bums; let Caleb hoise 'em;
Then apply Alecto's whip,
Till they wriggle, howl, and skip.

(ll. 181–390, in *Poems*, 519)

In the 'Preface' of *A Tale of a Tub* general satirists are satirized as impotent pedants:

> I have observ'd some Satyrists to use the Publick much at the Rate that Pedants do a naughty Boy ready Hors'd for Discipline: First expostulate the Case, then plead the Necessity of the Rod, from great Provocations, and conclude every Period with a Lash. Now, if I know any thing of Mankind, these Gentlemen might very well spare their Reproof and Correction: For there is not, through all Nature, another so callous and insensible a Member as the *World's Posteriors*, whether you apply to it the *Toe* or the *Birch*. (*PW* i. 29)

Swift's satire on the body politic artfully combined the general with the topical particular and seemed to imply specific menaces, as reflected in 'To a Lady', where all wicked politicians are arraigned, but Walpole is in the satirist's sights:

When my muse officious ventures
On the nation's representers:
Teaching by what golden rules,
Into knaves they turn their fools:
How the helm is ruled by Walpole,
At whose oars, like slaves, they all pull:
Let the vessel split on shelves;
With the freight enrich themselves:
Safe within my little wherry,
All their madness makes me merry:
Like the watermen of Thames,
I row by, and call them names.
Like the ever-laughing sage,
In a jest I spend my rage.

(Though it must be understood,
I would hang them if I could:)

(ll. 165–80, in Poems, 519)

This is satire with real world menaces. Swift wishes Whig politicians dead not mended. The parenthetical aside to the reader that he would kill the Whig leaders if he had them in his power is repeated elsewhere in Swift's poetry, where the circumstances that would enable it to happen are made a bit more explicit. In his poem 'The Revolution at Market Hill' Swift imagines himself and the Jacobite soldier Henry Leslie fellow 'sufferers in a ruined cause' who 'ventured to be hanged' in attacking the Whigs, mounting a successful local insurrection and being empowered to hang their opponents (*Poems*, 396–8). The parenthesis reminds us that when the joking is over Swiftian satire wishes its victims dead not mended. 'To a Lady' also significantly, if obliquely, in lines 174–8, acknowledges Swift's debt or allegiance as satirist to the learned Anglican satirist Robert Burton 'Democritus Junior', author of that great satiric cento *The Anatomy of Melancholy*.[2]

In his prose Swift perfected a concise, plain style – concrete diction and straightforward sentence construction – though he hardly practised plain statement. His prose is characteristically ironic and parodic, even at its plainest and most 'realistic'. When Gulliver says he 'chose to relate plain Matter of Fact in the simplest Manner and Style', the passage in fact parodies the claims made by contemporary voyagers and the linguistic prescriptions of the Royal Society at the time (IV. xii. 291). This assertion of plain-speaking, literal veracity at the end of a narrative containing little people, giants, flying islands, and rational horses, while outrageously maintaining the formal pretence that these are genuine and not lying travels, serves to subvert the notion that plain language provides a transparent window on reality. Swift's poetry has been characterized as anti-poetic, as plain and realistic. But here too Swift's 'realism' has much to do with reference to other texts and allusive recurrence. The factuality of even Swift's most 'realistic' poems such as 'A Description of the Morning' (1709; *Poems*, 107–8) or 'Holyhead. September 25, 1727' (*Poems*, pp. 329–30) is interconnected with other poems. Swift's device in his urban eclogue

'A Description of the Morning' of treating 'low' quotidian subjects within a classical frame, and indeed even the occasional observed 'realistic' detail, are anticipated, for example, in Charles Cotton's 'Morning Quatrains'.[3] 'Holyhead. September 25, 1727' was written as Swift waited for a boat to Ireland, where his friend Esther Johnson lay mortally ill. Swift's surroundings reflect his distress and despair. The poem begins:

> Lo here I sit at Holyhead
> With muddy ale and mouldy bread:
> All Christian victuals stink of fish,
> I'm where my enemies would wish.
>
> (ll. 1–4)

The landscape 'on this bleaky shore' expresses his mood: 'Where neither herb nor tree will thrive, | Where nature hardly seems alive' (ll. 29, 31–2). Swift's use of the pathetic fallacy here, however, recalls seventeenth-century poetic antecedents, especially another Anglican Dean John Donne's use of the device in his solemn poem occasioned by the death of his wife, 'A nocturnall upon S. Lucies day, Being the shortest day' (ll. 5–8: 'The worlds whole sap is sunke: | ... life is shrunke, | Dead and enterr'd').[4] Cotton's *The Wonders of the Peake* begins with the speaker seeing himself as an outcast figure damned 'to a place':

> Where *Nature* only suffers in disgrace.
> A *Country* so deform'd, the *Traveller*
> Would swear those parts Natures *pudenda* were:
> Like *Warts* and *Wens*, hills on the one side swell,
> To all but *Natives* inaccessible;
> Th'other a blue scrofulous scum defiles,
> Flowing from th'earths impostumated boyles ...
>
> (ll. 5–12)[5]

Cotton's scatological factuality here also anticipates another characteristic of Swift's satiric poetry.

Swift is notorious for his so-called scatological or excremental group of poems and perhaps his most infamous exhibit of the excremental poetic kind is 'The Lady's Dressing Room' (1732), one of Swift's most popular poems (*Poems*, 448–52, 827). In the poem, Strephon enters Celia's dressing room in Celia's

absence and while Betty the maidservant is 'otherwise employed' (l. 6). An *'inventory'* follows of the noisome detritus of
Celia's body and boudoir, in what can be read as a scatological
parody of Belinda's toilette scene at the end of Canto 1 in
Pope's *The Rape of the Lock*. The discovery of the true
nauseating nature of 'divine *Belinda*'s Chamber' was a topos of
demystification in seedy contemporary anti-feminist satire.[6]
The climax of Swift's poem is Strephon's discovery that 'Celia
shits', which deranges him. The poem deliberately and suc-
cessfully upset its first readers. Laetitia Pilkington said her
mother vomited when she read it (*Swift*, iii. 688). Swift
anonymously published *A Modest Defence of a Late Poem By an
Unknown Author, Call'd, The Lady's Dressing-Room* (1732), which
audaciously claims that this indecent poem is innocuous in
comparison to Horace's writing on the subject and contends
that the excremental satire merely recommends cleanliness
(*PW* v. 337–40). The poem provoked vigorous answers. In Lady
Mary Wortley Montagu's poem 'The Reasons that Induced Dr
S[wift] to write a Poem Call'd the Lady's Dressing Room'
(1734) we learn that Betty is employed in prostitution and
Swift is the punter. The Whig aristocrat pillories the Tory priest
in an imperfect enjoyment poem. Swift appears as an anal
retentive, vain, name-dropping fop. Swift detested triplet
rhymes. In Montagu's poem the impotent Swift's sexual failure
with Betty is highlighted in the poem's only triplet.[7]

'The Lady's Dressing Room' is a parody of the witness of the
Creation in book III of Milton's epic *Paradise Lost*. Uriel's
account of God's creation reads:

> I saw when at his word the formless mass,
> This world's material mould, came to a heap:
> Confusion heard his voice, and wild uproar
> Stood ruled, stood vast infinitude confined;
> Till at his second bidding darkness fled,
> Light shone, and order from disorder sprung
>
> (bk. III, ll. 708–13)[8]

In Swift's poem, Strephon finds Celia's room was 'void'. The
'matter' in the room is aggressively inventoried. Petticoats are
in 'frowzy heaps'. The savvy narrator advises Strephon to 'stop
his nose' and witness the cosmetic creation from foul chaos:

> When Celia in her glory shows,
> If Strephon would but stop his nose,
> Who now so impiously blasphemes
> Her ointments, daubs, and paints and creams;
> Her washes, slops, and every clout,
> With which she makes so foul a rout;
> He soon would learn to think like me,
> And bless his ravished eyes to see
> Such order from confusion sprung,
> Such gaudy *tulips* raised from *dung*.
>
> (ll. 135–44, in *Poems*, 452)

This parody of Milton is not often recognized, because Swift's ironic allusion to book III, lines 708–13, is not signalled (unlike another allusion to *Paradise Lost* at line 98 of Swift's poem, where the line appropriated from Milton (*Paradise Lost*, ii. 891) is put in quotation marks: '"Those secrets of the hoary deep"'). Swift's allusion to *Paradise Lost*, iii. 708–13, has the quality of a private ironic joke, for the first word in Milton's poem immediately after the passage to which Swift alludes is 'Swift' (see *Paradise Lost*, iii. 714).

Swift's satire certainly insists on artificial Celia's cloacal reality. But Swift's satire is not just about exposing the excremental reality masked by the cosmetic appearance, for the satire recommends, in its unillusioned way, the necessity of keeping up false appearances. 'Cosmetic' stems from the Greek word *kosmos*, meaning order and adornment. Swift's satire dismantles with violent intent, but redress for the defective body can be found in artificial adornment and concealment. In part II of *Gulliver's Travels*, Gulliver says he found the natural smell of the Brobdingnagian Maids of Honour 'supportable' even though it was offensive, but 'when they used Perfumes' he 'immediately swooned away' (II. v. 118–19). The nude Houyhnhnm master says to Gulliver that he had 'begun to think it not unwise in us to *cover* our Bodies, and by that Invention, conceal many of our Deformities from each other, which would else be hardly supportable' (IV. vii. 260). The savvy narrator of 'The Lady's Dressing Room' advises the use of aromatherapy. Strephon is to stop his nose, like Gulliver does when in company with his wife at the end of the *Travels* (IV. xii. 295). In *A Tale of a Tub* a defence of artifice and illusion is advanced. The stripped beau reveals 'many unsuspected Faults under one Suit of Cloaths'. An art that can 'sodder and patch up the Flaws and Imperfections of Nature, will deserve much better of Mankind' than exposing and anatomising them (*PW* i. 109–10). Another poem from the scatological group emphasizes that puppeteers must hide the fact that their noble characters are but made of wood and wire ('Strephon and Chloe', ll. 285–92, in *Poems*, 462). The dismembered nymph in 'A Beautiful Young Nymph Going to Bed', when the mechanical operation of dismantling her is completed, is shown to be only artifice. From artificial hair, mouse-hide eyebrows, and wired false teeth down there is almost no natural body at all, though just enough flesh to feel the 'pains of love' – that is, venereal disease. The tropes of love poetry have been literalized as prosthetical devices (her 'crystal eye'). There would be no woman at all if not for cosmetic 'art' (*Poems*, 453–5). At the end of 'The Lady's Dressing Room' the narrator counsels fatuous Strephons to be grateful for the spectacle of cosmetically created Celias. There are close similarities between the narrator's attitude and Swift's. In a letter to Esther Johnson in December 1711 Swift explained how he was to see a lady 'who is just up after lying-in; and the ugliest sight I have seen, pale, dead, old and yellow, for want of her paint. She has turned my stomach. But she will soon be painted, and a beauty again' (*PW* xvi. 443). More generally, this declared preference for appearance to a corrupt or noisome reality can be noticed throughout Swift's writings, expressed, for example, in the mock-argument preferring the outside to the inside of corporeal beings in *A Tale of a Tub* (*PW* i. 109), in the approval of a 'Livery of Religion' rather than open infidelity and vice in *A Project for the Advancement of Religion* (PW ii. 57) and in some of his 'Thoughts on Religion' (*PW* ix. 261–2), and in the defence of nominal Christianity, even when the real thing is absent, in *An Argument against Abolishing Christianity*.

As incongruous as it might seem, Swift was an (albeit cynical) advocate of cosmetics, and part of a curious Anglican counter-discourse to the more usual moralistic condemnation of cosmetics as sinful. Robert Burton's *The Anatomy of Melancholy* considered *'Artificial Allurements of Love'* and was a repository of learned views on the question as to 'whether natural or artificial objects be more powerful'. Burton opined that 'as it is used, artificial is of more force, and much to be preferred'.[9] John Gauden, Bishop of Worcester and the ghost writer of *Eikon Basilike*, the book said to have been written by King Charles the martyr, was also the reputed author of a discourse in favour of the use of cosmetics and those 'mechanick Arts' and artificial aids (false teeth, noses, hair, eyes made of glass or painted crystal, and so on) that seek to 'conceal, cover and supply Nature's grosser Deformities and Defects'. This clerical advocate of the cosmetic observes that Art daily makes 'those things which are but excremental, to be *ornamental* to our Bodies'. However, the aim of cosmetic art should be to make the person pleasing, decent, and neat, not to give the semblance of youth and beauty to the aged. There is no place for patching, mending, painting, polishing, and pruning 'our *Gibeonitish* Carcases, those rotten Posts, which are mouldring themselves away'.[10] The Royalist cleric Robert Herrick's *Hesperides* contains poems approving cosmetic art and expressing delighted acceptance of female illusionism. Such poems cohabit with lyrics proclaiming that some women with false breasts, teeth, hair, and eyes are only their artificial parts.[11]

Swift's scatological poems have been read, in his own time and since, as symptomatic transcripts of a personal pathology. However, they can be recognized as powerful and idiosyncratic interventions in a contemporary and traditional cultural discourse that was saying that it is probably just as well that the human carcass is covered up. The great Renaissance essayist Michel de Montaigne wrote, in his long sceptical essay 'Apology for Raymond Sebond', 'that we are the only animal whose defectiveness offends our own fellows, and the only ones who have to hide, in our natural actions, from our own species'. Montaigne considers it 'a fact worthy of consideration' that (the Ovidian) 'remedy to amorous passions' is 'the entire and open sight of the body that we pursue'. He observes that it 'is not so much modesty as artfulness and prudence that makes our ladies so circumspect in refusing us entry to their boudoirs before they are painted and dressed up for public display'. An observation supported by a quotation from Lucretius.[12] Swift invades the boudoir, inventories in excremental detail, and then counsels circumspection and staying outside to admire the illusory public spectacle.

Swift wrote several poems about himself. The most famous of these autobiographical poems is *Verses on the Death of Dr Swift, D.S.P.D.*, written in 1731 and published while he was still alive (see *Poems*, 485–98, 846–57). Swift produced his own post-mortem on his life and work. The poem presents a winning public-relations version of himself and apologia for his art: an image of a patriot, original writer, and fearless moral satirist. It is at the same time saying something different from what it appears to be saying, for irony and dubiety lurk behind apparently plain statements about the writer and his work. For example, as is now well known, the couplet declaring his originality (ll. 317–18) is stolen from John Denham's *On Mr Abraham Cowley* (see *Poems*, 854). In a poem entitled 'Whitshed's Motto on his Coach' Swift wondered about the hated Whig Lord Chief Justice Whitshed's family motto 'Liberty and my native country': '*Libertas & natale solum*; | Fine words; I wonder where you stole 'em' (ll. 1–2, in *Poems*, 282). Swift said of himself in *Verses*: 'Fair LIBERTY was all his cry; | For her he stood prepared to die' (ll. 351–2). His fine words are 'stolen' from the Royalist poet John Denham's praise of Charles I, a politically indicative 'borrowing' or 'homage', as I have indicated. Swift's irony in these cases does not cancel the literal claim. Swift's statements about himself elsewhere indicate that he very probably meant it when he said that he was an original writer and a patriotic champion of liberty, but perhaps he did not mean it in quite the way he hoped innocent readers would take it. Similarly the claim in *Verses* that Swiftian satire spares the victims' names (l. 464) is obviously contradicted by the personal satire in this very poem and by even a passing acquaintance with Swift's satiric works.

Verses presents a Swift with several identities rather than an identikit version that leads to a conviction about him. The poem itself exists in multiple versions. In the poem Swift speaks of himself in the first and third person and the information is doctored. The poem, in fact, has very little to say about his writings in verse and prose; we learn little about his personal life, about his family, about his relations with women, or indeed about his life before he worked for the Tory government. The lacunae found in the text and notes of the eighteenth-century editions of the poem in a way symbolize the fact that much about Swift can only be inferred or is absent altogether from the extant textual remains. The corpus of writing that does remain is notoriously difficult to negotiate, as are the original contexts in which the works reacted. When his greatest satiric hits *A Tale of a Tub* and *Gulliver's Travels* were delivered to the London printers, Swift had absconded from the scene of publication. We are still looking for the missing author and searching for signposts in his radically ironic works.

Notes

CHAPTER 1. BIOGRAPHY: PRIEST AND SATIRIST

1. *The Dunciad*, bk. I, ll. 19–22, in *The Poems of Alexander Pope: A One-Volume Edition of the Twickenham Text*, ed. John Butt (London, 1963), 721.
2. Obituary of Swift, *The True Patriot*, no. 1 (5 Nov. 1745), in Kathleen Williams (ed.), *Swift: The Critical Heritage* (New York, 1970), 109.
3. Swift's autobiographical account of his early life, 'Family of Swift', can be read at *PW* v. 187–95. It includes an event 'that seems very unusuall', his apparent abduction by his nurse, who took him from Dublin to Whitehaven and looked after him there for three years, his mother sending orders that the nurse was not to hazard a return voyage (*PW* v. 192). Sir William Temple's father 'had been a great Friend to the Family', and in 1689, after staying with his mother then in Leicester, Swift was received by Sir William Temple into his Moor Park household (*PW* v. 193).
4. John Boyle, Fifth Earl of Cork and Orrery, *Remarks on the Life and Writings of Dr Jonathan Swift*, ed. João Fróes (1751; Newark, NJ, 2000), 83.
5. Ralph Gray, 'The Coronation Ballad' (1689), ll. 61–71, in *Poems on Affairs of State: Augustan Satirical Verse, 1660–1714*, v. *1688–1697*, ed. William J. Cameron (New Haven, 1971), 44; [John Sergeant], *An Historical Romance of the Wars, between the Mighty Giant Gallieno, and the Great Knight Nasonius, and his Associates* (Doublin, 1694), 37–8.
6. *The Art of Assassinating Kings . . .* (London, 1696), 71–2, 88–91, 96, 98.
7. Ian Higgins, *Swift's Politics: A Study in Disaffection* (Cambridge, 1994), 53; Craig Rose, *England in the 1690s: Revolution, Religion and War* (Oxford, 1999), 156–7, 160.

8. André Breton, *Anthology of Black Humor*, trans. Mark Polizzotti (San Francisco, 1997), 3–17; Claude Rawson, 'Preface', in Jonathan Swift, *Directions to Servants* (London, 1995), p. x.

9. Arthur S. Marks, 'Seeking an Enduring Image: Rupert Barber, Jonathan Swift, and the Profile Portrait', *Swift Studies*, 16 (2001), 31–82, see esp. p. 76 and plate 15; Geoffrey B. Seddon, *The Jacobites and their Drinking Glasses* (Woodbridge: Antique Collectors' Club, 1995), 97–8 (on the rose and oak leaf emblems).

10. *A Letter to the Reverend Mr Dean Swift* ... (London, 1719), 16; Anthony Collins, *A Discourse concerning Ridicule and Irony in Writing* (London, 1729; repr. New York, 1970), 39; *An Author to Be Let ... by ... Iscariot Hackney*, in *The Works of Richard Savage, Esq. Son of the Earl of Rivers*, 2 vols. ([London], 1777), ii. 265. For modern assessments, see Roger D. Lund, 'Swift's Sermons, "Public Conscience," and the Privatization of Religion', *Prose Studies*, 18 (1995), 150–74, and Michael DePorte, 'Swift, God, and Power', in Christopher Fox and Brenda Tooley (eds.), *Walking Naboth's Vineyard: New Studies of Swift* (Notre Dame, Ind., 1995), 73–97.

11. For the ideology of religious intolerance informing the writings of High Churchmen, see Mark Goldie, 'The Theory of Religious Intolerance in Restoration England', in O. P. Grell, J. Israel, and N. Tyacke (eds.), *From Persecution to Toleration* (Oxford, 1991), 331–68, and his 'John Locke, Jonas Proast and Religious Toleration 1688–1692', in J. Walsh, C. Haydon, and S. Taylor (eds.), *The Church of England c. 1689–c. 1833* (Cambridge, 1993), 143–71.

12. *Verses on the Death of Dr Swift*, ll. 351–2, in *Poems*, 494; John Denham, *Coopers Hill*, ll. 325–6, in *Expans'd Hieroglyphicks: A Critical Edition of Sir John Denham's Coopers Hill*, ed. Brendan O Hehir (Berkeley and Los Angeles, 1969), 159.

13. *The Works of Mr Thomas Brown*, 4 vols. (4th edn.; London, 1715), i. 30; Daniel Defoe, *The True-Born Englishman. A Satyr*, 'The Preface', in *The True-Born Englishman and Other Writings*, ed. P. N. Furbank and W. R. Owens (Harmondsworth, 1997), 24.

14. Claude Rawson, *God, Gulliver, and Genocide: Barbarism and the European Imagination, 1492–1945* (Oxford, 2001), esp. pp. 266–75.

15. On this point, see Claude Rawson, 'Introduction', in *The Basic Writings of Jonathan Swift* (Modern Library College Edition; New York, 2002), pp. xxiii–xxiv.

16. On the London spectacle of a prostitute being flayed, see Ned Ward, *The London Spy* (1698–1700), ed. Paul Hyland from the Fourth Edition of 1709 (East Lansing, 1993), pt. VI, 102, 110. Swift's '*Anatomy*' (*PW* i. 110) here might be compared with Robert

Burton's *Anatomy of Melancholy*, pt. 3, sect. 2, memb. 5, subs. 3, where Chrysostom is quoted on a woman's beauty as a superficial skin that, when taken off, reveals 'all loathsomeness under it'; see Robert Burton, *The Anatomy of Melancholy*, ed. Holbrook Jackson, introduction William H. Gass (New York, 2001), 212; Prem Nath, 'The Background of Swift's Flayed Woman', *Forum for Modern Language Studies*, 20 (1984), 363–6. On the stripped beau, compare the account of '*A Beau*' in *The London Spy*, pt. XVI, p. 295: 'His body's but a poor stuffing of a rich case, like bran in a lady's pincushion, that when the outside is stripped off, there remains nothing that's valuable. His head is a fool's egg . . . His brains are the yolk, which conceit has addled.'

17. Joseph Hall, *Virgidemiarum*, iv. i. 43–4, in *The Collected Poems of Joseph Hall, Bishop of Exeter and Norwich*, ed. A. Davenport (Liverpool, 1949), 50. On Pope's praise of Hall, see p. xxvii n. 5.
18. See Vaughan Hart, 'Vanbrugh's Travels', *History Today*, 42 (July 1992), 26–32.
19. Sir John Vanbrugh, *The Provoked Wife*, ed. Antony Coleman (The Revels Plays; Manchester, 1982), 54.
20. On the rough justice and illiberal nature of Swift's satiric generalization, see Daniel Eilon, *Factions' Fictions: Ideological Closure in Swift's Satire* (Newark, NJ, 1991), esp. pp. 128–33.

CHAPTER 2. *A TALE OF A TUB*

1. See Kathleen Williams (ed.), *Swift: The Critical Heritage* (New York, 1970), 36.
2. Ibid. For the view of the book as irreligious, see William Wotton's hostile 'Observations' at pp. 37–46.
3. *The Complete Works of William Diaper*, ed. Dorothy Broughton (London, 1952), pp. xxvi–xxvii, 38.
4. See Frank Boyle, *Swift as Nemesis: Modernity and its Satirist* (Stanford, 2000), on Swift's particular satire of Bentley, Wotton, and especially Newton.
5. See also ibid. 144.
6. Ibid. 136.
7. See Ian Higgins, *Swift's Politics: A Study in Disaffection* (Cambridge, 1994), 62–74.
8. For an extended and more fully documented account of Swift's response to Dryden, see Ian Higgins, 'Dryden and Swift', in *John Dryden (1631–1700): His Politics, His Plays, and His Poets* ed. Claude Rawson and Aaron Santesso (Newark, NJ, 2004), pp. 217–34.

9. [Thomas Brown], *The Late Converts Exposed; or the Reasons of Mr Bays's Changing his Religion. Considered in a Dialogue. Part the Second* (London, 1690; repr. New York, 1974), 2–4, 17, 22.
10. *The Works of John Dryden*, ed. H. T. Swedenberg, Jr., et al., 20 vols. (Berkeley and Los Angeles, 1956–2000), iii. 119, 121, 131.
11. *The Hind and the Panther*, pt. II, ll. 533–7, 376–7, in ibid. iii. 155, 150.
12. Ibid. v, p. vii. See also Robert Phiddian, *Swift's Parody* (Cambridge, 1995), 128.
13. B. S. Johnson, *The Unfortunates*, intro. Jonathan Coe (London, 1999), 'Note' on the inside of the box; J. Hillis Miller, *Topographies* (Stanford, 1995), 6.

CHAPTER 3. SHORTER SATIRIC WORKS

1. *Merlinus Liberatus: Being an Almanack for the Year of our Blessed Saviour's Incarnation 1708 . . . by John Partridge . . .* (London, [1708]).
2. This account of the mock-astrological hoax draws on: Herbert Davis, 'Introduction', *PW* ii, pp. x–xiv; Richard P. Bond, 'John Partridge and the Company of Stationers', *Studies in Bibliography*, 16 (1963), 61–80, and his 'Isaac Bickerstaff, Esq.', in Carroll Camden (ed.), *Restoration and Eighteenth-Century Literature* (Chicago, 1963), 103–24; George P. Mayhew, 'Swift's Bickerstaff Hoax as an April Fools' Joke', *Modern Philology*, 61 (1964), 270–80; *Swift*, ii. 197–209; Margaret Weedon, 'Bickerstaff Bit, or, Merlinus Fallax', *Swift Studies*, 2 (1987), 97–106.
3. Mayhew, 'Swift's Bickerstaff Hoax as an April Fools' Joke', 270.
4. See Bond, 'John Partridge and the Company of Stationers', 61–80.
5. On Ward and Brown, see Benjamin Boyce, *Tom Brown of Facetious Memory: Grub Street in the Age of Dryden* (Cambridge, 1939), 129–33 and *Swift*, ii. 199; *Advertisements from Parnassus. Written Originally in Italian. By the Famous Trajano Boccalini. Newly Done into English, and adapted to the Present Times . . . by N.N. Esq* (London, 1704), advertisement XXXV, 134.
6. Charles Leslie, *The Socinian Controversy Discuss'd, in Six Dialogues: Wherein the Chief of the Socinian Tracts Publish'd of Late Years, are Consider'd*, in *The Theological Works of the Reverend Mr Charles Leslie*, 2 vols. (London, 1721), i. 205.
7. For a contemporary exposition of Socinian doctrine, see the Socinian Stephen Nye's *A Brief History of the Unitarians, Called also Socinians*, first published without licence in 1687 and in an enlarged 2nd edn. in 1691. On Socinianism and its political–

theological impact, see H. John McLachlan, *Socinianism in Seventeenth-Century England* (London, 1951): for Nye, see pp. 320–2, for Locke and Newton, see pp. 327–8, 335; J. A. I. Champion, *The Pillars of Priestcraft Shaken: The Church of England and its Enemies, 1660–1730* (Cambridge, 1992), esp. pp. 106–32; J. C. D. Clark, *English Society 1660–1832: Religion, Ideology and Politics during the Ancien Regime* (Cambridge, 2000), 324–422 *passim*.

8. [Charles Leslie], *The Charge of Socinianism against Dr Tillotson Considered* (Edinburgh, 1695), 13–14, 32.

9. See esp. Leslie, *Works*, i. 212–21.

10. John Toland, *Christianity not Mysterious* (1696), 83.

11. *Advertisements from Parnassus*, advertisement XCI, 113.

12. Charles Leslie, *The Socinian Controversy Discuss'd: Wherein the Chief of the Socinian Tracts (Published of Late Years Here) Are Consider'd* (London, 1708), 37.

13. *The Trinitarian Scheme of Religion concerning Almighty God*, 7–8, in *A Second Collection of Tracts, Proving the God and Father of Our Lord Jesus Christ, the Only True God* (London, 1693).

14. Stephen Nye, *A Brief History of the Unitarians Called Also Socinians* (n.p., 1687), 168-69; Matthew Tindal, *A Letter to the Reverend the Clergy . . . concerning the Trinity . . .* (n.p., 1694), 6, 16.

15. *A Discourse concerning the Nominal and Real Trinitarians* (n.p., 1695), 18.

16. [John Hildrop], *A Letter to a Member of Parliament, Containing a Proposal for Bringing in a Bill to Revise, Amend or Repeal Certain Obsolete Statutes, Commonly Called the Ten Commandments* (London: R. Minors, in St Clement's Church Yard, in the Strand, 1738), 5.

17. Ian Higgins, *Swift's Politics: A Study in Disaffection* (Cambridge, 1994), 190–2.

18. [Andrew Michael Ramsay], *An Essay upon Civil Government . . .* (London, 1722), 98.

19. George Wittkowsky, 'Swift's *Modest Proposal*: The Biography of an Early Georgian Pamphlet', *Journal of the History of Ideas*, 4 (1943), 88–9. For important studies of *A Modest Proposal* in the context of Swift's other writings on the Irish poor, see Claude Rawson, 'A Reading of *A Modest Proposal*', in his *Order from Confusion Sprung: Studies in Eighteenth-Century Literature from Swift to Cowper* (London, 1985), 121–44 (paperback edn., New Jersey, 1992), and David Nokes, 'Swift and the Beggars', *Essays in Criticism*, 26 (1976), 218–35. *A Modest Proposal* is one of the exemplary texts in Claude Rawson's examination of exterminatory rhetoric in *God, Gulliver, and Genocide: Barbarism and the European Imagination, 1492–1945* (Oxford, 2001).

20. [Bernard Mandeville], *A Modest Defence of Publick Stews . . . Written by a Layman* (London, 1724; repr. The Augustan Reprint Society, no. 162, intro. by Richard I. Cook, Los Angeles, 1973), 15.
21. *Swift*, iii. 162.
22. For a recent comparative study of Swift and Mandeville, see Claude Rawson, 'Mandeville and Swift', in Howard Weinbrot *et al.* (eds.), *Eighteenth-Century Contexts: Historical Inquiries in Honor of Phillip Harth* (Madison, 2001), 60–80.
23. See Daniel Eilon, *Factions' Fictions: Ideological Closure in Swift's Satire* (Newark, NJ, 1991), esp. pp. 40–2.
24. For examples known to Swift, see Jonathan Swift and Thomas Sheridan, *The Intelligencer*, ed. James Woolley (Oxford, 1992), 197–203 (*Intelligencer*, no. 18, 26–30 Nov. 1728, by Sheridan). There are also sources for the cannibalism topos, known or available to Swift, in travel literature, the Bible, the writings of the Church Fathers, and in classical literature: see Dirk F. Passmann, ' "Many Diverting Books of History and Travels" and *A Modest Proposal*', *Eighteenth-Century Ireland*, 2 (1987), 167–76.
25. *The Works of Jonathan Swift*, ed. by Walter Scott, xviii (Edinburgh, 1814), 26.
26. See Rawson, *God, Gulliver, and Genocide*, esp. pp. 79–91, 276, 285, and notes.
27. Ned Ward, *The London Spy*, 4th edn. of 1709, ed. Paul Hyland (East Lansing, 1993), no. XVI, 293.
28. See Gilly Lehmann, 'Politics in the Kitchen', *Eighteenth-Century Life*, 23 (1999), 71–83 and her references.
29. *Advices from Parnassus. By Trajano Boccalini. Translated from the Italian. With Observations, Reflections, and Notes* [by Matthias Earbery] (London, 1727), advice IV, p. 16. Swift had read this work (*Corr.* iii. 227–8).
30. Flavius Josephus, *The Jewish War*, v. 248–9; 515–41; vi.193–213, in *Josephus*, ed. and trans. H. St. J. Thackeray, 9 vols. (Loeb Classical Library; London, 1928), iii. 277–81, 361–7, 433–7. Roger L'Estrange's contemporary English translation of Josephus went through many editions and was abridged as *The Wars of the Jews . . . with the Most Deplorable History of the Siege and Destruction of the City of Jerusalem*. The translation was in print and popular in the 1720s and would have been familiar to many readers, as Swift's pamphlet assumes.
31. Rawson, *God, Gulliver, and Genocide*, 25–6.

CHAPTER 4. *GULLIVER'S TRAVELS*

1. On Swift's use of travel literature, see Arthur Sherbo, 'Swift and Travel Literature', *Modern Language Studies*, 9 (1979), 114–27; Dirk Friedrich Passmann, *'Full of Improbable Lies': Gulliver's Travels und die Reiseliteratur vor 1726* (Frankfurt am Main, 1987).
2. Lionel Wafer, *A New Voyage and Description of the Isthmus of America*, ed. L. E. Elliott Joyce (Oxford, 1934), 19.
3. Ibid. 6.
4. William Dampier, *A Voyage to New Holland . . .* (London, 1703), 147.
5. William Dampier, *A New Voyage Round the World . . .* (5th edn., London, 1703), 464; Dampier, *A Voyage to New Holland*, 148.
6. Charles Leslie described the independent 'state of nature' imagined in Whig political theory in his account of the 'Hottentots' in *A Battle Royal between Three Cocks of the Game. Mr Higden, Hoadly, Hottentote. As to the State of Nature and of Government*, appended to his *The Finishing Stroke. Being a Vindication of the Patriarchal Scheme of Government . . .* (London, 1711), 125–239. Like Swift with the Houyhnhnms, Leslie uses the idea of a primitivist state of nature illustrated in the Hottentots to satirize modern European luxury and corruption. However, Leslie's Hottentot reveals that the state of nature supposed by John Locke and others is a fictional fantasy and that the Hottentot's actual natural state is hierarchical, patriarchal, and absolutist. It is contended that monarchy or family government is found everywhere on earth.
7. [Andrew Ramsay], *An Essay upon Civil Government* (London, 1722), 36, 37; Swift, *Verses on the Death of Dr Swift*, l. 41, in *Poems*, 486.
8. [Ramsay], *An Essay upon Civil Government*, 30, 32.
9. John Boyle, Fifth Earl of Cork and Orrery, *Remarks on the Life and Writings of Dr Jonathan Swift* (1752), ed. João Fróes (Newark, NJ, 2000), 180.
10. *The Duke of Wharton's Reasons for Leaving his Native Country, and Espousing the Causes of his Royal Majesty King James III. In a Letter to his Friends in Great Britain and Ireland* (n.p., [1726]), 7–8; Ian Higgins, 'Jonathan Swift and the Jacobite Diaspora', in Hermann J. Real and Helgard Stöver-Leidig (eds.), *Reading Swift: Papers from the Fourth Münster Symposium on Jonathan Swift* (Munich, 2003), 87–103.
11. See Richard Savage, 'Britannia's Miseries' (1716), ll. 100–4, in *The Poetical Works of Richard Savage*, ed. Clarence Tracy (Cambridge, 1962), 23; *The True Briton*, no. XX (9 Aug. 1723), in *The Life and Writings of Philip Late Duke of Wharton*, 2 vols. (London, 1732), i. 173.

12. *The True Briton*, no. 61 (30 Dec. 1723), in *The Life and Writings of Philip Late Duke of Wharton*, ii. 523; Ramsay, *An Essay upon Civil Government*, 65–6; Matthias Earbery, *Advices from Parnassus. By Trajano Boccalini*, no. IV (London, 1727), advice XVIII, p. 86. See also Murray Pittock, *Inventing and Resisting Britain: Cultural Identities in Britain and Ireland, 1685–1789* (Basingstoke, 1997), 91–5.

13. Robert Burton, *The Anatomy of Melancholy*, ed. Holbrook Jackson, introduction by William H. Gass (New York, 2001), pt. I, sect. 3, memb. 1, subs. 2, p. 396.

14. Ibid., pt. 2, sect. 4, mem. 1, subs. 3, p. 217.

15. Strephon is advised to 'stop his nose,| Who now so impiously blasphemes' about Celia in 'The Lady's Dressing Room' (ll. 136–7, in *Poems*, 452).

16. I am referring to characteristic claims in 'soft' readings of *Gulliver's Travels*. For the contours of the critical controversy about part IV, see James L. Clifford, 'Gulliver's Fourth Voyage: "Hard" and "Soft" Schools of Interpretation', in Larry S. Champion (ed.), *Quick Springs of Sense* (Athens, Ga., 1974), 33–49. I am presenting a 'Hard School' reading in this book.

17. On the frontispiece portraits, see Janine Barchas, 'The Paratext of *The Travels*: Gulliver's Many Faces', in Jonathan Swift, *Gulliver's Travels*, ed. Albert J. Rivero (Norton Critical Edition; New York, 2002), 467–80. See also Jenny Mezciems, 'Utopia and "the Thing which is not"': More, Swift, and Other Lying Idealists', *University of Toronto Quarterly*, 52 (1982), 40–62; Peter Wagner, *Reading Iconotexts: From Swift to the French Revolution* (London, 1995), 37–73.

18. Boyle, *Remarks on the Life and Writings of Dr Jonathan Swift*; Daniel Wavell on *Gulliver's Travels*, in Joseph Spence, *Observations, Anecdotes, and Characters of Books and Men: Collected from Conversation*, ed. James M. Osborn, 2 vols. (Oxford, 1966), i. 393.

19. On the frontispiece portraits that taken together present Gulliver as like and unlike Swift, see Barchas, 'The Paratext of *The Travels*'. The best reading of the interplay between Swift and Gulliver to which I am indebted is Claude Rawson, 'Gulliver and Others: Reflections on Swift's "I" Narrators', in Swift, *Gulliver's Travels*, ed. Rivero, 480–99.

20. *Advertisements from Parnassus. Written Originally in Italian. By the Famous Trajano Boccalini. Newly Done into English, and adapted to the Present Times . . . By N.N. Esq* (London, 1704), advertisement XLVI, 176.

21. On Gulliver as Swift's Noah or Lot and the presence of the Old Testament Book of Genesis, and other Books in Swift's writing,

see Claude Rawson, *God, Gulliver, and Genocide: Barbarism and the European Imagination, 1492–1945* (Oxford, 2001), esp. pp. 266–75, 298–310.

22. *Gulliver Decypher'd* (London, n.d.), 38.

23. *The Life of Aristides the Athenian, Who was Decreed to be Banish'd for His Justice . . .* (Dublin: Printed by Daniel Tompson, 1714), 25.

24. *The Duke of Wharton's Reasons for Leaving his Native Country*, esp. pp. 3, 7–8.

25. Ian Higgins, 'Jonathan Swift and the Jacobite Diaspora', in Real and Stöver-Leidig (eds.), *Reading Swift*, 90.

26. Dampier, *A Voyage to New Holland*, 89–90.

27. *The Poems of Alexander Pope*, ed. John Butt (London, 1963), 486–8.

28. Kathleen Williams (ed.), *Swift: The Critical Heritage* (New York, 1970), 65.

29. See also Denis Donoghue, *Jonathan Swift: A Critical Introduction* (Cambridge, 1969), 19–22.

30. *Cato's Letters*, no. 67, 24 Feb. 172[2], in John Trenchard and Thomas Gordon, *Cato's Letters or Essays on Liberty, Civil and Religious, and Other Important Subjects*, ed. Ronald Hamowy, 4 vols. in 2 (Classics on Liberty; Indianapolis, 1995), 474.

31. Rawson, 'Gulliver and Others: Reflections on Swift's "I" Narrators', 496.

32. R. S. Crane, 'The Houyhnhnms, the Yahoos, and the History of Ideas', in J. A. Mazzeo (ed.), *Reason and the Imagination: Studies in the History of Ideas, 1600–1800* (New York, 1962), 231–53; Samuel Butler, *Hudibras*, ed. John Wilders (Oxford, 1967), First Part, Canto 1, ll. 65, 71–2, p. 3; Rochester, 'Tunbridge Wells', ll. 180–6; 'A Satyre against Reason and Mankind', ll. 1–7, in *The Works of John Wilmot, Earl of Rochester*, ed. Harold Love (Oxford, 1999), 53–4, 57.

33. Benjamin Boyce, *Tom Brown of Facetious Memory* (Cambridge, Mass., 1939), 84–5.

34. John Richardson, 'Alexander Pope's *Windsor Forest*: Its Context and Attitudes toward Slavery', *Eighteenth-Century Studies*, 35 (2001), 1–17.

35. Deborah Baker Wyrick, '*Gulliver's Travels* and the Early English Novel', in Peter J. Schakel (ed.), *Critical Approaches to Teaching Swift* (New York, 1992), 132–48 (pp. 141–8).

36. For the presence of Ancient Sparta in *Gulliver's Travels*, first noted by Orrery and expounded by W. H. Halewood and other modern scholars, see the evidence brought together in Ian Higgins, 'Swift and Sparta: The Nostalgia of *Gulliver's Travels*', *Modern Language Review*, 78 (1983), 513–31.

CHAPTER 5. POEMS

1. Claude Rawson, 'Introduction', in *The Basic Writings of Jonathan Swift*, selected with an Introduction by Claude Rawson, Notes by Ian Higgins (Modern Library; New York: 2002), pp. xviii–xxii.
2. Some of Swift's many borrowings from and echoes of Burton's *Anatomy* are recorded in the Notes to the Modern Library edition of *The Basic Writings of Jonathan Swift*. Swift's lines seem to recall a contemporary anecdote (by White Kennett published in 1728) about Burton: *'Yet I have heard that nothing at last could make him laugh, but going down to the Bridge-foot in Oxford, and hearing the Barge-men scold and storm and swear at one another, at which he would set his Hands to his Sides, and laugh most profusely'*, quoted in Nicolas K. Kiessling, *The Legacy of Democritus Junior Robert Burton* (Oxford, 1990), 99.
3. Compare the last line of 'A Description of the Morning': 'And schoolboys lag with satchels in their hands', with 'Morning Quatrains', ll. 65–6: 'The slick-fac'd School-boy Sachel takes, | And with slow pace small riddance makes'. Swift and Cotton are parodying a conventional descriptive detail. Swift's 'Betty' and 'Moll' with her mop have analogues in *'Kate'* with her pail in 'Morning Quatrains', l. 39, or *'Madg*, the dirty Kitchin-Quean' in 'Night Quatrains', l. 54: see *Poems of Charles Cotton*, ed. John Buxton (London, 1958), 1–5, 11.
4. *Donne Poetical Works*, ed. Herbert J. C. Grierson (Oxford, 1929; paperback edn., Oxford, 1971), 40.
5. *Poems of Charles Cotton*, 52.
6. *The Works of Mr Thomas Brown, Serious and Comical, In Prose and Verse*, 4 vols. (4th edn.; London, 1715), iii. 152–4.
7. Lady Mary Wortley Montagu, *Essays and Poems and Simplicity, A Comedy*, ed. Robert Halsband and Isobel Grundy (Oxford, 1993), 273–6.
8. John Milton, *Paradise Lost*, ed. Alastair Fowler (London, 1971), 187. See Ian Higgins, 'An Allusion to *Paradise Lost* in Swift's "The Lady's Dressing Room"', *ANQ* 2 (Apr. 1989), 47–8.
9. Robert Burton, *The Anatomy of Melancholy*, ed. Holbrook Jackson, introduction William H. Gass (New York, 2001), pt. 3, sect. 2, memb. 2, subs. 3, p. 88 and *passim*.
10. [John Gauden, Bishop of Worcester], *Several Letters between Two Ladies: Wherein the Lawfulness and Unlawfulness of Artificial Beauty in Point of Conscience, Are Nicely Debated. Published for the Satisfaction of the Fair Sex* (London, 1701), 48, 52–3, 56, 85–6. I wish to thank Dr Valerie Rumbold for drawing my attention to this work.

11. Robert Herrick, *Hesperides* (1648; Scolar Press facsimile, Menston, 1969). Compare 'Painting sometimes permitted' (p. 263) and 'Upon Julia's Clothes' (pp. 307–8) with 'Upon some women' (pp. 84–5).
12. *The Complete Essays of Montaigne*, trans. Donald M. Frame (Stanford, 1965), bk. II, ch. 12, pp. 356–7.

Select Bibliography

There is a vast scholarly archive on Jonathan Swift that continues to grow steadily. The following is a very short list of books on Swift. The emphasis is on books published or republished since 1990 that may be accessible in large public and university libraries. Recent work of course builds on earlier scholarship. The listed bibliographical works would enable a comprehensive coverage of the critical production on Swift.

STANDARD MODERN EDITIONS

The Correspondence of Jonathan Swift, ed. Harold Williams, 5 vols. (Oxford, 1963–5).

The Correspondence of Jonathan Swift, D.D., ed. David Woolley, 4 vols. (Frankfurt am Main, 1999–).

Jonathan Swift: The Complete Poems, ed. Pat Rogers (Harmondsworth, 1983).

The Poems of Jonathan Swift, ed. Harold Williams, 3 vols. (2nd edn.; Oxford, 1958).

The Prose Writings of Jonathan Swift, ed. Herbert Davis *et al.*, 16 vols. (Oxford, 1939–74).

A new scholarly edition: *The Cambridge Edition of the Works of Jonathan Swift*. General Editors: Ian Higgins, Claude Rawson, David Womersley, Textual Editor: James McLaverty is in preparation.

ANNOTATED EDITIONS OF INDIVIDUAL WORKS

A Discourse of the Contests and Dissentions between the Nobles and the Commons in Athens and Rome, ed. Frank H. Ellis (Oxford, 1967).

The Drapier's Letters, ed. Herbert Davis (Oxford, 1935).

Gulliver's Travels, ed. Paul Turner (World's Classics; Oxford, 1998).
Gulliver's Travels, ed. Robert DeMaria, Jr. (Penguin Classics; Harmondsworth, 2001; rev. 2003).
Gulliver's Travels, ed. Albert J. Rivero (Norton Critical Edition; New York, 2002).
The Intelligencer, ed. James Woolley (Oxford, 1992).
Journal to Stella, ed. Harold Williams, 2 vols. (Oxford, 1948; repr. as vols. xv and xvi of *The Prose Writings of Jonathan Swift*).
Memoirs of Martinus Scriblerus (with Pope, Arbuthnot, Gay, *et al.*), ed. Charles Kerby-Miller (New Haven, 1950; reissued Oxford, 1988).
Polite Conversation, ed. Eric Partridge (London, 1963).
Swift vs. Mainwaring: 'The Examiner' and 'The Medley', ed. Frank H. Ellis (Oxford, 1985).
A Tale of a Tub, ed. A. C. Guthkelch and D. Nichol Smith (2nd edn.; Oxford, 1958; corrected reprint, 1973).
A Tale of a Tub and Other Works, ed. Angus Ross and David Woolley (Oxford, 1986).

BIBLIOGRAPHY

Landa, Louis A., and Tobin, James Edward, *Jonathan Swift: A List of Critical Studies Published from 1895 to 1945* (1945; repr. New York, 1975).
Rodino, Richard H., *Swift Studies, 1965–1980: An Annotated Bibliography* (New York, 1984).
Stathis, James J., *A Bibliography of Swift Studies 1945–1965* (Nashville, 1967).
Teerink, H., and Scouten, Arthur H., *A Bibliography of the Writings of Jonathan Swift* (2nd. edn.; Philadelphia, 1963).
Vieth, David M., *Swift's Poetry 1900–1980: An Annotated Bibliography* (New York, 1982).
The Scriblerian (1968–). A periodical that is published twice a year (with a cumulative Bibliography and Index every five years). Gives annotated coverage of work on Swift.
Swift Studies: The Annual of the Ehrenpreis Center, ed. Hermann Real (1986–). A specialist journal devoted to Swift that also lists recent work. 'A Supplemental Bibliography of Swift Studies, 1965–1980' by Richard Rodino, Hermann J. Real and Heinz J. Vienken appeared in *Swift Studies*, 2 (1987), 77–96.
www.jaffebros.com/lee/gulliver/ The best current worldwide web site for Swift (with an up-to-date bibliography section).

SWIFT'S LIBRARY

LeFanu, William, *A Catalogue of Books belonging to Dr Jonathan Swift Dean of St Patrick's, Dublin Aug. 19. 1715: A Facsimile of Swift's autograph with an introduction and alphabetic catalogue* (Cambridge Bibliographical Society Monograph, no. 10; Cambridge, 1988).

Williams, Harold, *Dean Swift's Library. With a Facsimile of the Original Sale Catalogue and Some Account of Two Manuscript Lists of his Books* (Cambridge, 1932).

BIOGRAPHY

Arnold, Bruce, *Swift: An Illustrated Life* (Dublin, 1999). A provocative and readable account of enigmatic aspects of Swift's biography.

Boyle, John, Fifth Earl of Cork and Orrery, *Remarks on the Life and Writings of Dr Jonathan Swift*, ed. João Fróes (Newark, NJ, 2000). Orrery's *Remarks* (1751) is the first critical biography on Swift and inaugurates a tradition of overheated reaction to Swift's misanthropy.

Ehrenpreis, Irvin, *Swift: The Man, his Works, and the Age*, 3 vols. (London, 1962–83). The standard, comprehensive modern biography.

Elias, A. C., Jr., *Swift at Moor Park: Problems in Biography and Criticism* (Philadelphia, 1982). Detailed account of Swift's time with Sir William Temple when Swift was at work on *A Tale of a Tub*.

McMinn, Joseph, *Jonathan Swift: A Literary Life* (Basingstoke, 1991). A concise account.

Nokes, David, *Jonathan Swift, A Hypocrite Reversed: A Critical Biography* (Oxford, 1985). An unsettling account of Swift's life, particularly acute on his relations with friends and protégés.

CRITICISM

General Studies

Boyle, Frank, *Swift as Nemesis: Modernity and its Satirist* (Stanford, 2000).

Crook, Keith, *A Preface to Swift* (London and New York, 1998). Useful reference material; an example of the hostile reading of the Houyhnhnms in part IV of *Gulliver's Travels*.

Eilon, Daniel, *Factions' Fictions: Ideological Closure in Swift's Satire* (Newark, NJ, 1991).

106

Kelly, Ann Cline, *Jonathan Swift and Popular Culture: Myth, Media, and the Man* (New York, 2002)

Montag, Warren, *The Unthinkable Swift: The Spontaneous Philosophy of a Church of England Man* (London, 1994).

Rawson, Claude, *Gulliver and the Gentle Reader: Studies in Swift and our Time* (London, 1973; paperback edn., New Jersey, 1992).

—— *Order from Confusion Sprung: Studies in Eighteenth-Century Literature from Swift to Cowper* (London, 1985; paperback edn., New Jersey, 1992).

Williams, Kathleen (ed.), *Swift: The Critical Heritage* (London, 1970). A collection of eighteenth- and early nineteenth-century responses to Swift.

Collections of Essays

Connery, Brian A. (ed.), *Representations of Swift* (Newark, NJ, 2003).

Douglas, Aileen, Kelly, Patrick, and Ross, Ian Campbell (eds.), *Locating Swift: Essays from Dublin on the 250th Anniversary of the Death of Jonathan Swift, 1667–1745* (Dublin, 1998).

Fox, Christopher (ed.), *The Cambridge Companion to Jonathan Swift* (Cambridge, 2003).

—— and Tooley, Brenda (eds.), *Walking Naboth's Vineyard: New Studies of Swift* (Notre Dame, Ind., 1995).

Freiburg, Rudolf, Loffler, Arnö, and Zach, Wolfgang (eds.), *Swift: The Enigmatic Dean: Festschrift for Hermann Josef Real* (Tübingen, 1998).

Rawson, Claude (ed.), *Jonathan Swift: A Collection of Critical Essays* (New Century Views; Englewood Cliffs, NJ, 1995).

Schakel, Peter J. (ed.), *Critical Approaches to Teaching Swift* (New York, 1992).

Wood, Nigel (ed.), *Jonathan Swift* (Longman Critical Readers; London, 1999).

Papers from the major international Swift symposia held at Münster in Germany have been published as books by Wilhelm Fink Verlag, edited by Hermann Real and others (1985, 1993, 1998, 2003).

Church and Politics

Cook, Richard I., *Jonathan Swift as a Tory Pamphleteer* (Seattle, 1967).

Downie, J. A., *Jonathan Swift: Political Writer* (London, 1984). A critical biography that focuses on Swift's political sensibility.

Fauske, Christopher J., *Jonathan Swift and the Church of Ireland, 1710–1724* (Dublin, 2002)

Higgins, Ian, *Swift's Politics: A Study in Disaffection* (Cambridge, 1994).

Landa, Louis A., *Swift and the Church of Ireland* (Oxford, 1954).

Lock, F. P., *Swift's Tory Politics* (London, 1983).

Swift and Ireland

Fabricant, Carole, *Swift's Landscape* (Baltimore, 1982; Notre Dame, Ind., 1995).

Ferguson, Oliver W., *Jonathan Swift and Ireland* (Urbana, Ill., 1962).

McMinn, Joseph, *Jonathan's Travels: Swift and Ireland* (Belfast, 1994).

—— (ed.), *Swift's Irish Pamphlets: An Introductory Selection* (Gerrards Cross, 1991).

Mahony, Robert, *Jonathan Swift: The Irish Identity* (New Haven, 1995).

A Tale of a Tub

Craven, Kenneth, *Jonathan Swift and the Millennium of Madness: The Information Age in Swift's 'A Tale of a Tub'* (Leiden, 1992).

DePorte, Michael, *Nightmares and Hobby Horses: Swift, Sterne, and Augustan Ideas of Madness* (San Marino, 1974).

Harth, Phillip, *Swift and Anglican Rationalism: The Religious Background of 'A Tale of a Tub'* (Chicago, 1961).

Paulson, Ronald, *Theme and Structure in Swift's 'Tale of a Tub'* (New Haven, 1960).

Phiddian, Robert, *Swift's Parody* (Cambridge, 1995). Focuses on pre-1714 works and especially *A Tale of a Tub*.

Smith, Frederik N., *Language and Reality in Swift's 'A Tale of a Tub'* (Columbus, 1979).

Gulliver's Travels

Erskine-Hill, Howard, *Jonathan Swift: Gulliver's Travels*, Landmarks of World Literature (Cambridge, 1993).

Fox, Christopher (ed.), *Jonathan Swift, Gulliver's Travels* (Case Studies in Contemporary Criticism; Boston, 1995). Reprints the standard Davis text of *Gulliver's Travels* with critical essays from various theoretical perspectives.

Hammond, Brean, *Gulliver's Travels* (Open Guides to Literature; Milton Keynes and Philadelphia, 1988).

Lock, F. P., *The Politics of 'Gulliver's Travels'* (Oxford, 1980).

Smith, Frederik N., ed., *The Genres of Gulliver's Travels* (Newark, NJ, 1990).

Tippett, Brian, *Gulliver's Travels*, The Critics Debate (Basingstoke and London, 1989).

Poems

Fischer, John Irwin, *On Swift's Poetry* (Gainesville, Fla., 1978).

Fischer, John Irwin, and Mell, Donald C. (eds.), *Contemporary Studies in Swift's Poetry* (Newark, NJ, 1981).

Jaffe, Nora Crow, *The Poet Swift* (Hanover, NH, 1977).

Johnson, Maurice, *The Sin of Wit: Jonathan Swift as a Poet* (Syracuse, NY, 1950).

Pollak, Ellen, *The Poetics of Sexual Myth: Gender and Ideology in the Verse of Swift and Pope* (Chicago, 1983).

Schakel, Peter J., *The Poetry of Jonathan Swift* (Madison, 1978).

CULTURAL CONTEXTS

Black, Jeremy (ed.), *Culture and Society in Britain 1660–1800* (Manchester, 1997).

Hammond, Brean S., *Professional Imaginative Writing in England, 1670–1740: 'Hackney for Bread'* (Oxford, 1997).

Levine, Joseph M., *The Battle of the Books: History and Literature in the Augustan Age* (Ithaca, NY, 1991).

Rawson, Claude, *God, Gulliver, and Genocide: Barbarism and the European Imagination, 1492–1945* (Oxford, 2001).

Rawson, Claude, *Satire and Sentiment 1660–1830* (Cambridge, 1994; New Haven, 2000).

Rogers, Pat, *Grub Street: Studies in a Subculture* (London, 1972). Abridged as *Hacks and Dunces: Pope, Swift, and Grub Street* (London, 1980).

HISTORICAL CONTEXTS

Black, Jeremy, and Porter, Roy (eds.), *The Penguin Dictionary of Eighteenth-Century History* (1994; Harmondsworth, 1996).

Boyce, D. George, Eccleshall, Robert, and Geoghegan, Vincent (eds.), *Political Discourse in Seventeenth- and Eighteenth-Century Ireland* (Basingstoke, 2001).

Champion, J. A. I., *The Pillars of Priestcraft Shaken: The Church of England and its Enemies 1660–1730* (Cambridge, 1992).

Clark, J. C. D., *English Society 1660–1832: Religion, Ideology and Politics during the Ancien Regime* (2nd edn., Cambridge, 2000).

Connolly, S. J., *Religion, Law and Power: The Making of Protestant Ireland, 1660–1760* (Oxford, 1992).

Cruickshanks, Eveline, *The Glorious Revolution* (British History in Perspective; Basingstoke, 2000).

Harris, Tim, *Politics Under The Later Stuarts: Party Conflict in a Divided Society 1660–1715* (London and New York, 1993).

Hill, Brian, *The Early Parties in Britain, 1688–1832* (Basingstoke, 1996).

Holmes, Geoffrey, *British Politics in the Age of Anne*, rev. edn. (London, 1987).

Hoppit, Julian, *A Land of Liberty? England 1689–1727* (Oxford, 2000).

Moody, T. W., and Vaughan, W. E. (eds.), *A New History of Ireland*, iv. *Eighteenth Century, 1691–1800* (Oxford, 1986).

Pittock, Murray G. H., *Jacobitism* (Basingstoke, 1998).

Rose, Craig, *England in the 1690s: Revolution, Religion and War* (Oxford, 1999).

110

Index

111